WHEN I LOOK
INTO THE MIRROR
AND SEE YOU

WHEN I LOOK
INTO THE MIRROR
AND SEE YOU

WOMEN,
TERROR, AND
RESISTANCE

Margaret Randall

Rutgers University Press
NEW BRUNSWICK, NEW JERSEY, AND LONDON

The title of this book is based on a line from the song "Walls and Windows," written in 1984 by the North American songwriter and singer Pat Humphries and the Australian songwriter and singer Judy Small. This song was sung by thousands of women at the opening session of the International Women's Forum in Beijing in the summer of 1996.

Library of Congress Cataloging-in-Publication Data

Randall, Margaret, 1936–
    When I look into the mirror and see you : women, terror, and resistance / Margaret Randall.
        p. cm.
    Includes bibliographical references.
    ISBN 0-8135-3184-5 (cloth : alk. paper)
    ISBN 0-8135-3185-3 (pbk. : alk. paper)
        1. Women political activists—Violence against—Central America.
    2. Women political activists—Central America—Interviews.
    3. Women—Central America—Social conditions.   4. Women—
    Violence against—Central America.   I. Title.

HQ1236.5.C35 R26 2003   2002017878

British Cataloging-in-Publication information is available from the British Library.

Manufactured in the United States of America

There are no innocents among the disappeared.
Every one of them was guilty of wanting a better world.

Carlos Caillabet

CONTENTS

ACKNOWLEDGMENTS

My deepest gratitude goes to Nora Miselem Rivera and María Suárez Toro, who trusted me to listen to their story and to tell it from my point of view. I expect both these extraordinary women will write their own stories when they are ready to take a break from living them. I am also grateful to W.O.M.E.N. (Women's Observer Mission to the Elections in Nicaragua: Building Our Political Power)—particularly Estelle Schneider and Jill Winegardner—for having created the space in which this story could be told and for supporting the project in all its stages. My gratitude to Kim Chernin, Marjorie Agosín, and Rutgers University Press editor Leslie Mitchner for suggestions that made this a better book. Thanks also to the Boehm Foundation, the late Carol Bernstein Ferry, GLUE (Gay and Lesbian Unity Education), Joy Hainsworth, Brigitte Hauschild, Lorraine Ironplow, the Money for Women / Barbara Deming Memorial Fund, Jane Norling, Puffin Foundation, Bob Schweitzer, Joyce Thomas, and W.O.M.E.N. for financial aid during the research and writing.

WHEN I LOOK
INTO THE MIRROR
AND SEE YOU

ONE

THE PRISM
WOMEN'S HUMAN RIGHTS

Language evokes, describes, communicates. But language can also be used to obscure and mislead. It can be used to kill. Today's political discourse, cynically manipulated, often does just that. Nowhere is this more evident than when speaking of violence. How do we define violence, who do we see as perpetrating it, which acts of violence do we condemn and which, if any, do we justify?

We call the Islamic fundamentalists who attacked the United States on September 11, 2001, terrorists. But when our government launches all-out war against the civilian population of the nation harboring other members of the terrorist group, it is routing out evil. Thousands of innocents are murdered, yet a co-opted use of language deems the attack an act of terrorism, the war a justified response.

The same is true in other scenarios. A man who rapes a woman may be said to be acting on natural instinct. Boys will be boys. If he knows the woman, he may be giving her what she asked for. When a father sexually abuses his daughter, it is often called a family issue, not warranting interference by the state. When an individual willfully causes another's death, it is murder; when the state executes the murderer, justice has been done. In some countries, young girls are routinely genitally mutilated; the practice is seen as a time-honored tradition rather than an act of terror.

Violence, like all other human interaction, is gendered: women and children are most often its victims, men or male-controlled states their victimizers.

1

Terrorism may be defined as the unwarranted attack upon one human being or group by another human being, group, or state. Governments, organizations, and individuals all perpetrate acts of terror. In modern times these have ranged from the mass genocide of the Nazi Holocaust, the United States's dropping of the atomic bomb on Hiroshima, or the years of apartheid in South Africa, to incidents in which an abusive husband murders his wife, a frustrated worker guns down his office colleagues, or a couple of deeply troubled high school students open fire on other students and teachers.

Those who hold the power name the act; they may define (and excuse) it as solving the Jewish problem, ending the war, keeping the race pure, seeing that justice is done, shooting up a school, or exercising control over a piece of property. Governments almost always define their own actions as just and necessary, individual acts of rebellion or frustration as terrorist.

In our societies, men have traditionally held the power. Women's lives are shaped and manipulated by male power, male laws. In the context of violence and terror, women are targeted in specific ways. Women also respond to this targeting with our own profoundly female insights and strengths. The human rights arena is no exception. Until the late 1980s, the movement was defined by those who proposed working in the area: white men from Western cultures. Today women—and women and men from other cultures—are broadening these definitions. The previously rigid separation between the public and the private is beginning to break down.

In recent years there has also been some discussion about which laws, policies, and acts should be considered terrorist. Is terrorism only defined as the sudden violent attack, the individual kidnapping, murder, battery, or rape? Is it justifiable (or even legal) to terrorize an enemy? Are political policies that indenture economies and starve whole populations, that condone mass lay-offs by companies whose CEOs make seven-figure salaries, and that deny medication to those who are poor and suffer from AIDS not also forms of terrorism? Are the millions of women and girls brutalized in their homes any less deserving of human rights protection than are their sisters who are more visibly victimized by repression or war?

Although most will agree that acts of individual lawlessness are terrorist in nature, the policies that keep communities or nations of people poor and hungry are rarely seen as such. At least not by the governments and corporations that promote these policies. On the other end of the spectrum, what fathers and husbands (and sometimes also mothers and grandmothers) do to children and to women is too often considered personal—not subject to public scrutiny.

There is state terrorism and the terror perpetrated one on one but by vast numbers of people. And there is the random terrorism carried out by individuals. The former affects much greater numbers of people than the latter, making it infinitely more dangerous and destructive. The more power the perpetrator wields, the greater the potential for damage. Yet most official and media attention is focused on the lone act—perhaps as a way of diverting our attention from the root problem.

The 1970s and 1980s in Latin America were decades of tremendous social unrest. From Guatemala to Haiti, from Bolivia to Argentina and Chile, people rebelled against years of impoverishment and injustice. Cuba had managed to sustain its successful 1959 revolution; the Sandinistas took power in Nicaragua in 1979. There was enormous fear, on the part of the United States and its allies, that other countries in Central and South America would choose similar ways out of ever-worsening poverty and despair.

Governments—many of them dictatorships installed through military coups—used increasingly violent methods of repression against the forces of opposition and the populations that supported them. Even when civil governments were voted into power, the military often retained behind-the-scenes control. The cold war mentality continued to nurture an obsessive anticommunism, and in almost every case, local armies and paramilitary groups were funded, trained, and supported by the United States. A succession of U.S. administrations backed terrorist governments that slaughtered, captured, disappeared, tortured, and murdered important segments of their own popula-tions—regimes, in short, that practiced mass genocide.

In Central America, during this period, military governments (no-tably in Guatemala, Honduras, and El Salvador) were guided by a doctrine of national security. This doctrine labeled as the enemy any person or social or political organization that called for social change. Even today, most of the Central American military establishment con-tinues to be shaped by this doctrine.

These regimes went after members of the opposition and those per-ceived as sympathizers. Armies, police, and paramilitary death squads massacred whole villages and towns. The death squads' sinister reach extended even to foreigners suspected of having links to those involved in these struggles for social change. In Guatemala and El Salvador, sev-eral dozen foreign priests and religious sisters were murdered. In the latter country, in March 1980, a beloved archbishop was assassinated while saying mass in the national cathedral. In December of that same year, four U.S. churchwomen were raped and killed. The victims of these years of state-imposed violence include women and men, priests and religious, labor leaders, peasants, students, academics, even chil-dren and the old.

All this—along with a new consciousness of human rights abuses throughout the world—provoked a reexamination of how those with power violate those without.

Perceptions of the rights of social classes and individuals have changed throughout history and are diverse today, depending on the particular culture. Only in the twentieth century have we spoken of a distinct category called human rights: rights considered basic, which every human should be able to take for granted—to life, personal safety, freedom of movement, religious belief, and political opinion.

At first these rights were said to apply to all men, and it was assumed that the term *mankind* somehow included women. This assumption is no longer made, at least not by feminists and others who see women as human beings in their own right.[1]

Class, race, ethnicity, religion, regional situation, and the existence of specific conflict were once the guidelines for looking at the issue of human rights. Only in the past couple of decades has it become clear that the issue of human rights, like most others, is also gendered. That is to say, women are viewed through the prism of our gender and discriminated against in particular ways. This understanding spawned a powerful movement specifically for women's human rights.

The patriarchal objectification of women has a long and complex history. It affects literally every aspect of our lives. Throughout Central and Latin America, the image of woman as virgin or whore is deeply woven into the social fabric of societies oppressed by the patriarchal dictates of the Catholic Church. Notwithstanding the differences inherent in distinct national cultures, Latin American women who do not conform to the traditional roles of dutiful daughter, obedient wife, caring mother, and long-laboring grandmother have been targets of derision, disrespect, and a broad spectrum of violence.

Over the past quarter century, individuals and groups of women throughout the continent have broken from these strictures in a variety of ways. Many joined with their brothers in the political struggles of the seventies and eighties. Their early roles were often limited to those of the traditional female sphere: hiding and feeding combatants, running messages, providing logistical support. Quickly, however, women began to challenge their male comrades' notions of what they could or could not do. Women themselves became fighters and took part in military operations, and not a few became political leaders (although very rarely are they found among the top echelons).

In Nicaragua, where I spent a number of years and wrote extensively about women's revolutionary participation, older women took risks and assumed roles unequaled by their male counterparts. There too I was witness to the many different ways in which women were beginning to challenge gender assumptions—even those presumably made with their best interests in mind.

An example of one such challenge can be seen in the case of a young woman captured during the Somoza era and raped in the dictator's torture chambers. She became pregnant from that rape. Although Nicaragua is a profoundly Catholic country and, even during the decade of Sandinista rule, abortion remained illegal, this woman's male comrades arranged for her to end the pregnancy; the child, after all, had been engendered by a torturer.

But this rape victim defied her comrades' plans for her unborn child. She saw the child not simply as a product of having been raped in torture but as a new life growing within her. It would be her child as well, primarily her child, she felt. And so she refused the abortion, confident that she could raise her son or daughter without shame for the baby's origin. As I spoke with this woman, now in freedom, her healthy happy young daughter played at her feet.

The objectification of women, the particular roles they are assigned, and male assumptions about their abilities, honor, needs, fears, weaknesses, and desires lead not only to the discrimination of overprotection or abuse in normal social situations but also to gender-specific treatment when they are captured and tortured. Rape and other forms of sexual abuse are often central features of women's torture.

In Latin America, women captured when pregnant were kept alive until their children were born, and those children were then delivered for adoption—often to childless families within the military apparatus. The mothers were then murdered. More than a quarter of a century later, heroic efforts are still being made to reunite these lost children with their grandparents.[2]

Repressive forces used women to try to compromise male leaders. In the clandestine prisons of Central and Latin America, cases of extreme gender-specific abuse have been documented.[3] In almost every culture, a particular set of mores exists around women, and these are always taken into account by the repressive forces. Women also seem to respond differently than men when their human rights are assaulted.

Once it became apparent that women's human rights must be considered as a category apart, progress toward defining the concept was determined and international in scope. The Rwanda Tribunal's recognition of rape in war as an act of genocide is an example of this progress. In a patriarchal world, however, opposition is strong. The terrible oppression of women in Afghanistan, although decried by feminists for a number of years, was not really noticed in any palpable way by the U.S. government until it had another reason to object to the Taliban: its support of al Qaeda, the terrorist network that attacked the United States in September 2001.

The 1993 World Conference on Human Rights in Vienna strongly affirmed the universality and indivisibility of women's rights as human rights. It explicitly recognized that violence against women and girls, in public and private, constitutes a serious human rights violation. After the Vienna conference came the Conference on Population and Development in Cairo, and then the Fourth World Conference on Women in Beijing. Both reaffirmed the Vienna commitment.

The problem, of course, has been how to turn commitments on paper into a reality for women throughout the world—where so many live in misery, subordination, and fear, and where patriarchal belief systems continue to keep women and girls isolated from their own potential. Charlotte Bunch, executive director of Rutgers University's Center for Women's Global Leadership, says that not only have we not advanced nearly enough, but we have fallen back: "Globalization for many women has so far meant that their rights are being narrowed by economic transitions, crisis, and cutbacks; growing numbers of women and girls are falling prey to international trafficking for purposes of economic and sexual exploitation. The past five years has brought an erosion of many women's right to health, education, freedom of movement and expression, and for some, even subordination to gender apartheid."[4]

Among a series of recommendations, Bunch urges the United Nations General Assembly and the governments of the world to take high-level action to ensure women's right to live free from violence. She points out that "Women and men who support women's human rights are being threatened, often violently, throughout the world—whether by killings of reproductive health care providers in the USA or attacks in the streets of Afghanistan," and she emphasizes that "women's rights are human rights," indeed that "human rights depend on women's rights."[5]

This story of two women, from two Central American countries, explores and highlights some of the gender-specific methods used with female prisoners, and also the creative forms of resistance they were able to develop—forms of resistance that helped them survive and ultimately led to their release.

Disappearance was among the most heinous of the weapons wielded by state terrorism in Latin America during the 1970s and 1980s. Of all the strategies for terrorizing individuals, families, and entire populations, disappearance may be the most psychologically damaging. In processes of political struggle, prisoners are removed from their loved ones. Families left without members—especially those members who provided economic support—must find other ways of surviving. The tortured, alone and cut off from their communities of support, suffer unimaginable agonies before they are murdered and their bodies relegated to unmarked graves. Remaining family members spend months, years, sometimes lifetimes, searching in vain for loved ones; their lives are forever changed.

Disappearance not only affects its victims in terrifying ways; it also provides an almost impermeable cover for those who perpetrate the crime. Denial is the order of the day. Trails leading to the whereabouts of victims end abruptly. Few mutilated bodies point a finger at the guilty. Mass graves are unearthed, if at all, many years after the fact—when statutes of limitations have run out or the murderers are safely ensconced in another life. In only a tiny percentage of cases have the guilty been charged, much less punished. Other dead are buried and may be grieved, but disappearance—a particularly Latin American twentieth-century form of terror—denies this necessary closure.

Now it is time to hear from the protagonists of this story.

By its very nature, there are few testimonies from the disappeared. This story, however, is an exception; it is a story of disappearance that found voice. It belongs to the women who lived it, but in a larger sense it belongs to all those committed to justice and concerned with creating a world in which justice thrives. It is important, among much else, for what it reveals about the brutality of repressive orders and about a people's resistance to that repression; it is important for what it tells us about the phenomenon of disappearance itself.

This is also a story about women's fortitude and courage, brilliance and decision—women's space and voice both during the events described and since. Nora's and María's individual stories open windows onto the realities of two Central American countries, Honduras and Costa Rica, and within those countries onto two women's extraordinary powers of resistance.

Fourteen years separate the living from the telling. During that time, each of the protagonists developed her own coping mechanisms, her own recipe for survival.

For a time, survival was posited upon silence.

Now it demanded voice.

A few words about my role. In transmitting this testimony, I acknowledge that the damage wrought by so much torture and death affects language itself. Perhaps there is no language capable of expressing the terror of mass tragedy as experienced by the peoples of Central and Latin America during the 1970s and 1980s. Faced with histories of unimaginable terror, people often say that a new language is needed to adequately describe such a phenomenon.

Torture, death, and disappearance, especially when they are perpetrated against so many and over such a long period of time, necessarily produce a rupture between the victims of that violence and the historic moment they were destined to inhabit. All the common references are gone. This alone makes the bridge of language more difficult to construct.

But poets and writers have often been able to construct these bridges. It falls to us to evoke a heretofore unimaginable reality in ways that may bring some measure of resolution to the survivors and reconnect the rest of us—and future generations—with vital chapters of our history. Perhaps the experience, in its passage through poetic imagery, allows us to feel extreme pain and suffering while keeping a certain distance from the resultant trauma.

The Uruguayan psychoanalyst Maren Ulriksen de Viñar says that "listening to these testimonies of horror is a way of breaking the silences, [of expressing] what could not be said: the words drowned by the torture itself. Raw testimony, a straightforward description of events, may prove unbearable: an obscene text."[6] For me, the testimonies of those who lived the experience have always been a necessary ingredient to the history's telling.

I am privileged to be able to offer the testimony that follows. I hope the circular organization of this book—perhaps more spiral than circle—will enable the reader to descend with these women into memory and emerge with them as they reclaim their experience and its meaning for us all.

TWO

NORA AND MARÍA

Nora Miselem Rivera is Honduran; María Suárez Toro a Puerto Rican who has lived for many years in Costa Rica. Their stories—and their combined story—break with traditions of silence, taboos that emerged in the political organizations of the times as well as within society as a whole.

Now these stories become A Story, one that is both unusual and ordinary. Readers of the story—with its references to clandestinity, kidnapping, disappearance, torture, and survival—may judge it in the former category. Its ordinariness becomes apparent as we learn that these women were attacked, and came very close to dying, for defending human dignity, and for teaching skills as basic as reading and writing, that they are both from the middle classes and are well educated, that their lives, in so many ways, are no different from ours.

Nora and María are two women among tens, perhaps hundreds, of thousands in Latin America who were disappeared by their country's repressive forces during the state-imposed terror of the 1970s and 1980s. They survived through a combination of tenacity, intelligence, and luck. And they were able to speak because a time, a place, and conditions all converged in a particular way.

It is important that we understand this.

These are women who have devoted their entire adult lives to working for social change. Not just working for it but positioning themselves on the front lines of grossly unequal struggles, making a conscious

11

choice to sacrifice what their societies consistently told them was success, and risking their lives to do so. Ironically, participating in these struggles for collective liberation often demanded a silence that inhibited personal liberation.

Nora and María participated in the political movements of the 1970s and 1980s, assuming—side by side with men—the difficult conditions and almost certain repression that characterized Latin America during those decades. Although other women shaped these women's lives in powerful ways, each out of her own particular background and history came to feminist consciousness through the experience of working with men.

The historical moment is also important here. What could not have been revealed in the eighties, when political structures demanded a rigid internal discipline, could be spoken about—had to be spoken about—a decade later, when it became painfully clear that real social change would not be possible under the forced silence of patriarchy. A gender analysis was needed, and for this analysis to be complete it had to include a gender perspective on struggle itself.

For this is not simply the story of two women. In a very palpable sense it is a story that belongs to all women—uttered because feminist consciousness has empowered us to speak out, and because women's space provided the safety necessary to its telling. Women who have come up articulating concepts of class and race now understand that gender and other previously ignored categories must also be factored into any successful equation for change.

In a larger, deeper sense, this story also belongs to men. If, finally, we are to create a world in which all of us can live, men must begin to claim women's experience, listen and learn. Men must allow the wisdom of women to shape their lives, as we have absorbed much of what is good—and a great deal of what is destructive—from them.

This is how Nora and María came upon one another again, fourteen years after their shared ordeal. The Sandinista National Liberation Front (FSLN) of Nicaragua ousted a long-standing dictatorship and took power in the summer of 1979. Many, elated by the FSLN's promise of a more just society, followed its progress closely. The Sandinistas remained in office ten years, eventually losing the elections of 1990 to a United States–backed coalition of mostly center-right parties. The brutal Contra war ended, but many of the exuberant social programs of the preceding decade also began to unravel. In October 1996, Nicaraguan presidential elections were once again about to take place.

Among the more than one thousand visitors from around the world was a group of women organized to observe those elections. We called ourselves W.O.M.E.N., Women's Observer Mission to the Elections in Nicaragua: Building Our Political Power. We would meet with local women's groups, civic organizations, and political parties. Then, accredited by Nicaragua's Supreme Electoral Council, we would visit the polling places and report on the electoral process.

As far as we knew, we were the first international all-woman contingent to monitor a presidential election. A small core group in the United States—composed of activists whose personal histories with Nicaragua and with Nicaraguan women compelled us to take on the challenge—managed to bring together forty-one women from eighteen countries. We came from South Africa, Eritrea, Croatia, the Philippines, the Dominican Republic, El Salvador, Guatemala, Mexico, and Canada. From Palestine, Switzerland, Panama, Zimbabwe, Haiti, Puerto Rico, and the United States. And from Honduras and Costa Rica. The protagonists of the story I am about to tell could not have suspected the ways in which their lives would be altered by the experience they were about to share—or how their story would affect those of us privileged to watch and listen.

The decade of the dirty wars was finally over. The wars were forgotten by the few in the United States who had known of their existence, and in those countries in which the shadow of a dirty war had dominated national life for so long, it was beginning to be erased from the minds of the younger generations. The current pressures on Central American peoples, as on the vast majorities in the developing world, were cloaked in the less dramatic but equally disempowering guises of globalization, structural adjustment, free trade agreements, and the other exigencies of neoliberal politics.

But the untold stories of those years continue to be relevant, because the same misery exists with an older more exhausted face, because we must retrieve our histories in order to remember who we are, and because—as Nora and María so convincingly tell us—when we look into the mirror we are all too likely to see another woman's face.

In 1996 Nora Miselem, Honduran mother of two, was in her mid-forties. She worked with the Center for the Rights of Women in Tegucigalpa. María Suárez, also in her forties, ran FIRE, the influential Feminist International Radio Endeavor broadcasting from Santa Ana, Costa Rica. A couple of days into their Managua stay, these women realized they knew one another—out of a terrible, intense, emotionally charged, and powerfully shared past.

A small sitting room off our hotel lobby. Several women sit talking. There is the doorway—I can see it still—and then, unexpectedly, framed within it is Nora, who has just arrived from the airport. María, inside the room, looks up. The two women's eyes meet, lock, are transformed. Quickly they are in one another's arms, laughing and crying at the same time.

Along with others on the delegation, I am shaken by Nora and María's rediscovery of one another. Their story touches us all. In suggesting and then organizing the following interview, I offer their memories beyond the magic circle our group became.

October in Managua. It is a typically hot and humid day. Accompanied by Liz Miller, who filmed the interview, and Holly Bowen Augusta who aided her, Nora, María, and I sit around a wooden table in the inner courtyard of one of the small hotels in Managua's San Juan district. The place is crowded with visitors; most, like us, are in the city for the elections. But it is as if we have this space to ourselves; no one comes near us, no one interrupts. Time does not move. It is late morning when we begin to talk, midafternoon when we stop. With minor changes, made for the sake of coherence and clarity, what follows is our initial conversation.

MARGARET: We're here in Managua, in the context of an extraordinary women's delegation—extraordinary women and an extraordinary delegation that brings us together. A few days ago I heard about the meeting between the two of you. This is the sort of thing that tends to happen among women, and I don't think it's coincidental. So I'd like you to tell me that story first: what happened to you a couple of days ago, and then what happened—when was it?—fourteen, fifteen years ago.

MARÍA: It was July 25 . . .

NORA: No, July 26, 1982. More than fourteen years.

MARGARET: Tell me what happened. Because I don't really know the story.

MARÍA: I'd like to start by talking about what happened the day before, because there's a reason I said July 25 just now. This meeting with Nora has brought up lots of memories I'd kept repressed, some perhaps in my subconscious, others even more deeply hidden, in my body's cells. I said July 25 and Nora said July 26 precisely because of something we talked about on our way to this interview.

On July 25, when I was in Tegucigalpa, after returning from the Salvadoran refugee camps in Honduras—where I and others had been organizing a literacy campaign—I was sitting in the plaza, right across from the DIN, the country's National Intelligence Office. And I remember witnessing something that hasn't been written about in the annals of the Central American struggles of those years, something that has to do with women's protest. It not only made an impression on me at the time; it also helped me defend myself in what I was about to experience.

I was sitting in the park, killing time before going to the Ticabus Hotel, or to a house where I would be able to spend the night before returning to Costa Rica the following day—I was living in Costa Rica then—and I saw a group of prostitutes from one of the dragnets that the Honduran army frequently carried out in the brothels back then. These women were demonstrating in front of the DIN. They were demanding indemnity, a percentage of the soldiers' salaries in order to be able to support their children, many of whom were the result of having been raped by those very soldiers, who routinely satisfied their sexual needs and desire for diversion with them.

This impressed me, because I knew that it reflected a protest that wasn't making the news. And it was a very powerful protest. Thinking about it later helped me defend myself from the threats of rape on the part of those same soldiers.

So okay Nora, why don't you talk about where we met on July 26?

NORA: Actually, we met a bit earlier, in Tegucigalpa, when you came to work in the refugee camps.

MARGARET: Excuse me Nora, did you belong to a particular political organization?

NORA: I worked for a human rights organization. We offered solidarity to refugees from the different Central American countries, especially those who had taken refuge in Honduras. In the context of that solidarity, for which Honduras has always distinguished itself, we'd founded something called COSPUCA: the Committee of Solidarity with the Peoples of Central America.

I don't know if we were naive, or just very radical, to openly use the word *solidarity* in the organization's name. Because to the government, and especially to the military, in those days the word *solidarity* had the worst sort of connotation; it was the same as communism. In any case, we founded COSPUCA, and through that organization we worked along the border with El Salvador.

Our dear friend here [gestures to María] came along, and we went to the refugee camps together. She went to do research and support work, and I was planning to stay on in the camps for a couple of months, to get away from the military repression. I thought I'd be in the camps for a while. Because before this I'd been going and coming back, going and coming back—we always had to transport food and other supplies.

And of course we were also involved in human rights work, publishing lists of the names of the Honduran soldiers who were raping children, murdering refugees, and so forth. The Honduran soldiers displayed the same cruelty as the Salvadoran National Guard. There really wasn't any difference between the two armies.

So that's what I'd been doing. It was very dangerous work, and there'd been some problems. My sister's house had been searched, and they'd accused her of having a stash of arms. According to the police, those weapons were supposed to have belonged to me. And so I planned on spending some time cooling off in one of the camps. I got there, and right away a soldier told me to register at the command post at the entrance to the camp.

I presented myself and that's when they detained me. Along with a German reporter—unfortunately I can't remember her name. I didn't speak much English, but with the little I knew I told her she'd be better off if she got away. They were throwing stones at her and insulting us both. I told her they were insulting her and that it would be better if she just left. And I asked her to tell someone that I was being held. They took me to Santa Rosa de Copán, to a military camp there, and around nine o'clock that night let me go.

[To María] That must have been July 24. You remained in the camps. And I left, with two armed soldiers tailing me. In a town like Santa Rosa de Copán at nine o'clock at night there was nothing going on. I tried to go to the priest's house, but no one opened the door, at least not quickly enough. I tried Caritas,[1] and the same thing happened. Finally I managed to check into a hotel, where these two soldiers spent the whole night trying to get me to come out. The only thing I could think of was, there was a Bible—in those days all the hotel rooms in Honduras had Bibles—and I stayed up all night reading it so I wouldn't fall asleep. I opened one of those wire coat hangers and had it ready too—the only thing I could use as a weapon if they decided to break into the room.

I called San Pedro Sula. I didn't say I had problems, just that I was in Santa Rosa de Copán, which was enough to let them know I was in trouble. Because COSPUCA had opened an office there, but we'd had to close it and move on to San Pedro Sula because of the intensifying repression in the area.

They were always breaking into that office, searching us without a warrant, following us. They tried pushing us into cars. Anyway, I was traveling with a woman who had never been to Tegucigalpa. Her name was Narcisa López, and unfortunately she was taken prisoner later along with me. After spending that night in Santa Rosa de Copán, we finally made it to Tegucigalpa. But we couldn't shake our tail. By this time the military had all our movements checked out, right? In those days, no matter what kind of work we were doing we always had to be careful, cover our tracks, dissimulate; anything could be considered subversive.

So on the morning of July 26, Narcisa López and I woke up in this apartment in Tegucigalpa, an apartment where people stayed who traveled back and forth from the refugee camps, foreigners as well as Hondurans.

We'd arrived around ten o'clock the night before, and we'd gotten a call that someone wanted to see us. The person said he was from the seminary. Since we worked closely with church people, we said okay.

I remember the guy asked to meet in a very out of the way place, but we said no. It would be better if we met somewhere else, we told him, on a street that's only for pedestrians. That is, there's no way for cars to enter, and we thought we'd be safer there. Plus it was only a block from the COSPUCA office.

We thought okay, we'll meet him there, and if this really is someone who wants to hear about the kind of work we're doing, we can always take him to our office. We believed he was from the church. But the minute we saw him, we said this guy has nothing to do with the church. He was drinking beer. One of those telltale faces you see all over Honduras, an obvious plant. And right away he began asking us about arms, that sort of thing. So we said: Let's go over to COSPUCA.

We went out into the street—that street where no traffic was allowed—and there was the car. The whole operation already set up.

Pedestrian street in Tegucigalpa, where Nora was kidnapped in 1982. Photograph by Margaret Randall.

Lots of men. I really didn't see what kind of car they put us in, because they blindfolded us right away; they began hitting us and shoving us into the vehicle. At that moment I didn't see faces but I could feel. In that repressive period you learned to feel things and know exactly what was going on, because all your defense mechanisms would come to the surface. I knew we were in danger. I remember telling Narcisa: Look, this is a kidnapping. Get away if you can. And tell someone what's happened.

I tried to keep walking. The only thing I saw was a store window, and I remember asking myself: if I throw myself against that window, will I be able to break it with my body? Trying to figure out what to do. Just then I caught sight of two young North American men, missionaries, one of those pair of Mormons who are everywhere in our country. And I went up to them and said: My name is Nora Miselem. I repeated my name. But they didn't understand. They just stood there with their mouths hanging open. Because right away the paramilitary operatives shouted: No! They didn't want me to be able to say anything.

That was when they grabbed me. They dragged me along the street, and one of them hit me on the head with his pistol. And they shoved me into the car. At first I thought Narcisa had managed to escape. But in the car I began to hear crying, and that's when I realized they'd taken her too.

This was the second time I'd been picked up like that. Back in November 1980—I think it was—when the elections for the National Assembly took place, they also detained me briefly. That time I remember something that affected me deeply. Because up to that point we hadn't heard of women being involved in the roundups, at least not that we were aware of. And that time I was kidnapped by several men and two women. It seemed incredible to me, that a woman could be involved in something like that. One of them drove the car. They were women who collaborated with the repressive forces in Honduras.

But this time it was all men. First they took us to a place, the vehicle made lots of turns, and they took us to a place. . . . But later we can talk about what happened to us there.

MARÍA: I was also organized back then. I was a university professor, at the University of Costa Rica, in the School of Education. In 1981 I'd just returned from more than two years working in Nicaragua's literacy campaign, an experience that had been extraordinarily important in my life. And in conjunction with some of the men and women—Salvadoran refugees in Costa Rica, who were also involved in solidarity work and were here in Nicaragua during the literacy campaign—the Salvadoran teacher's union, ANDES June 21st, asked me if I would spend the next few years helping them organize a literacy campaign that could be used in the refugee camps in which people fleeing several of the Central American countries were congregated.

I was able to legitimize that very complex work, which the Salvadoran teachers themselves were already carrying out, by designing a social action project at the University of Costa Rica. So I was working as a teacher. I organized the campaigns and trained grass roots teachers in each of the refugee camps in the various Central American countries in which they existed. And I was able to coordinate the work being carried out in Honduras and Nicaragua with the support of the United Nations High Commission for Refugees (ACNUR).

So I was basically involved in solidarity work. I was working with the Salvadoran teachers union, from which I also learned a great deal and under extremely adverse conditions, and when I went to Honduras to train grass roots teachers at the Mesa Grande camp I was also on a mission coordinated by ACNUR. I didn't work directly for the United Nations, but they had asked me to design something they were interested in, which later became the literacy manual they financed. So this, in a nutshell, is what brought me to Honduras in the summer of 1982.

I was fascinated by the work in the camps. Besides learning a great deal, I was able to bear witness to the particular adversity endured by the refugees, and by people like Nora who were involved in support work there. Being in those camps was almost like being in the middle of the war. And although a dirty war against the refugees was also being waged in Costa Rica, and the Salvadorans there also suffered at the hands of the United States and the Contras, in the cases of Honduras and Nicaragua the war was right out there in the open. It was a war aimed directly at the Salvadoran people.

On that trip I spent seven days in the camps. And when I returned to Tegucigalpa to catch the bus for Costa Rica, Nora had given me a key to an apartment where people in the solidarity movement stayed. Nora and I had met at the camp. She told me that it would be dangerous for me to stay by myself at the Ticabus Hotel, or at any hotel in Tegucigalpa for that matter. And, in a great gesture of solidarity, she'd given me a key to the apartment she's already mentioned.

I was relieved, because I didn't really know Honduras. I was traveling alone. I wasn't alone in the camps or in the work itself, but I was traveling alone. And so I was happy not to have to spend the night by myself in some cheap hotel. You could feel the tension in the air. You could feel it in your body, what was going on around you. To a certain extent I even sensed what was about to happen. I'd felt it on the bus. I'd actually had this feeling that something might happen, but I thought it might happen on the bus.

When I got to the apartment, I took out the key and inserted it in

House in Tegucigalpa, where María was kidnapped in 1982. Photograph by Margaret Randall.

the lock. The lock turned. I opened the door. And as I bent down to set my suitcase on the floor I felt the barrel of a gun, cold metal, on either side of my throat. I was looking down so I couldn't see, but as I raised my head—in that silence and with those gun barrels cold against my skin—I remember seeing the feet of several compañeros. They were men's feet, all of them, the feet of those in the apartment they had already captured, who were lying on the floor with guns also trained on them.

I tried to look around but the guns kept me with my neck and head down. And I don't know how, but I was able to get them to lower their guns by saying, right away: I have to go to the bathroom. And you know, I'd never been in that damned apartment before, but when they lowered their guns I made a beeline for the bathroom. Later, despite my denial, that would give them reason to accuse me of being familiar with the place.

The whole apartment was a mess. Total chaos. There must have been a dozen soldiers, and three or four compañeros on the floor, guns trained on them, and it was obvious they'd been beaten. The house had been torn apart. And I went straight to the bathroom!

In that bathroom with the door closed was where I managed to take stock, to try to think—well, I really didn't think anything; it was more a feeling about what was happening. I took as deep a breath as possible and tried to figure out what was going on. When I came out of the bathroom, that's when they began to question me, one question after another, fast, and I understood we were being taken into custody.

I was involved because I had the apartment key. I couldn't explain how it was that I had a copy of that key. I knew that Nora was being followed and that she'd been picked up once before. And I didn't want to mention anyone's name. The soldiers naturally assumed that I was part of the group, or was linked to it in some way, because I'd let myself in with that key. I'd never been there before. I had the address on a piece of paper. And then I'd headed straight for the bathroom.

Right away they demanded to know: Who are you? Someone said: Here's her passport. Look at it. And I said: I come from Costa Rica, I'm a teacher, I'm working in the refugee camps. And how did you come to this apartment, they asked, where did you get the key? That was the main thing. And I said: I got it in the camps, it's a key to an apartment that lots of people use. And in fact the United Nations High Commission for Refugees suggested I sleep here because it's very dangerous for a woman to stay alone in a hotel. And just look where the real danger turned out to be!

When they dragged us down to the waiting vehicle, that's when I felt Nora beside me. They blindfolded me right away, which is why I say I felt her. We were blindfolded with our hands tied, but they threw us into the truck, the same truck in which they'd brought you [to Nora] from somewhere else. At first I didn't know it was Nora, although I'd met her back at the camp. And of course the others I didn't know at all.

NORA: Remember, when we first met I said: Look what big ugly feet I have?

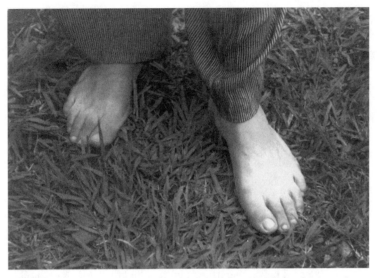

Nora's large feet, which helped María identify her in the clandestine prison, despite the fact that both women were blindfolded. Photograph taken in Tegucigalpa in April 1997, by Margaret Randall.

MARÍA: Yes, yes precisely!

NORA: In that first clandestine prison you recognized me because of my feet. Because I stuck my feet out when I realized there was someone there in front of me. I tried making contact with my feet.

MARÍA: Yes, because in the truck we couldn't see or talk and of course we couldn't say who we were. It's true, later, when we were in the first clandestine prison, I looked down and I asked myself: could those be your feet? Is that you, Nora? I remembered your name because of your feet. Because, of all the people I'd met, I knew those feet. That was our second meeting, when they threw us down tied up and blindfolded.

As Nora says, they took us for a real ride, lots of twists and turns. I didn't know Tegucigalpa at all. I didn't have any idea of where we were or where we were going. By that time I did have a pretty good idea of what was happening. And somehow, the fact that Nora was there, I mean she was the only one I knew, and the only one I knew who knew me. I didn't know the other compañeros at all. Not even the other woman.

MARGARET: And you scarcely knew each other, because you'd only just met.

MARÍA: Exactly. We'd met at the camp. And we'd talked. We coordinated what had to be coordinated around the literacy campaign. And that was that. But for me it was particularly important. Because with the other compañeros, well, my biggest problem was that they also didn't know how I'd happened to show up with that key in my hand. That was complicated. Because for quite a while the others there thought that I might be working with the army, infiltrated into the solidarity work in order to try to get information.

So, besides the fact that during the first few days we were all in solitary confinement—we could hear each other's screams, we could feel one another's presence—I was also in a cell right next to the bathroom. When the other prisoners were taken to the bathroom, that was when I could feel their movements and hear them talking. For me, besides the fact that I was being held in solitary confinement, the political isolation was the worst. And of course Nora couldn't talk to the others and explain who I was.

MARGARET: When they brought you to the first clandestine prison, that first day when they brought you there, did the interrogations begin immediately, the mistreatment, the torture?

MARÍA: First I want to talk a bit more, to insist on the fact of our bodily contact. Because they threw us all down, remember? Remember how they piled us into that truck, and as time passed we tried to make contact with one another's bodies, to help one another not feel so alone? And whenever one of us tried to say something, whatever we tried to say, I remember that right away: wham! That's when they brought the gun barrels down on us. They even tried separating us with the barrels of their guns. There in the truck was where it all began, the intimidation. And that's where we also began to use our physical contact to be supportive of one another. I don't remember much else.

The only thing I remember about that first night is that when we entered the clandestine prison — and I had no idea, they'd taken dozens of turns along the way, and if I'd been able to see I still wouldn't have known — that's when they separated us. Because they separated me. I really didn't know where the rest of the compañeros were. But it felt to me as if we were being separated. You get an image in your head, and you project from that. I was in solitary confinement so I thought everyone was.

NORA: You know, as I listen to you talk about your experience I'm understanding a little better. I wasn't in that group.

MARÍA: Ah . . .

NORA: Because, when they picked Narcisa and me up, they took us in a small car, not a truck. I know for sure she was next to me. They tore off a piece of my clothing and tied it over my eyes. And they kept me in a squatting position.

MARÍA: That must have been the second trip then.

NORA: Yes it was. After the little car they switched us over to a bus; I'm pretty sure it was a bus, because I was able to . . . I was lying in the aisle and I was able to touch the metal supports of the seats on either side. And I said: this is a large bus. And Narcisa was there beside me. And they were already taunting us, threatening us, asking about Father Fausto.

They would shove the barrels of their guns against our heads and pull the trigger, without the guns being loaded. Then they took us to the first clandestine cell. And when we got there, they separated Narcisa and me right away. I didn't know, I thought Narcisa was the only other woman they had.

As the days went by I began to realize . . . and that's when I stuck my feet out, so that you could see them. Because I remember one of the soldiers saying: Don't talk. That's when I realized there was someone else there. I was lying on the floor of a bathroom, my hands and feet were tied and I had a blindfold over my eyes. And I realized they had another prisoner in there with me. And I wanted that other prisoner to know that there were more of us. That's when I stuck my feet against the toilet, looking for contact with another human being.

I thought to myself, whoever it is will be able to see just about as much as I can. I tried to touch her, and I coughed. And they hit me again. I coughed so she would know I was there, would know someone else was there. But at that point I still didn't know it was you. I couldn't identify who it was. I just wanted whomever it was to know that there were more of us. It never occurred to me that the other comrades who'd gone to the apartment had also been picked up.

As soon as they brought me in, I was taken before one of the officers. And he interrogated me. He said: Okay, here's where you're going to talk. We don't waste time here. You're not going to find it easy in here; you're going to talk. And I said: Well, if you torture me I'll just have to invent things.

I still felt pretty strong. I was still able to use that resource, my strength. They knew my last name. It's Arabic and not a common name in Honduras. So I figured I'd take that tack. I could tell that the official wasn't all that educated; he was a low-level officer. And that's where it all began: the threats—this is where you'll have to talk, and so forth. That's when the interrogation itself began.

At first I thought I was alone. I knew Narcisa had been captured as well, but I thought they might be holding her somewhere else. I remember thinking about all the comrades who might have been in that room at one time or another. I thought about Tomás Nativí, Fidel Martínez, and so many others . . . compañeros—they'd disappeared. Had they been in this room where I was now? Maybe they were still there? No, I was sure that these monsters had already assassinated them.

Then they took me to another room, right there in the same house. And they began applying electric shocks to my feet, to my knees. They told me to open my mouth and stick out my tongue so they could put the wires there. But I wouldn't let them. They made me open my legs and began running the electricity to my vagina.

And they said: You bitch, women like you shouldn't be allowed to give birth. They said they were going to sterilize me, because I didn't deserve to have children—that idea they have of a woman as some sublime being whose sacred role is bearing children. According to them I was breaking with the tradition of what a woman was supposed to be. And they were going to punish me, from their point of view, so I wouldn't be able to have children. A woman like me didn't deserve to be a mother.

MARGARET: At that point you didn't have any children?

NORA: Well, that was another card they played. And it's one of the things that really affected me. I had given birth to a little boy, my first, but he had died at the age of two. He'd died just a couple of years before this, in 1980. And I was still dealing with that loss, trying to get over my little boy's death. So the psychological torture was well aimed. In fact, they said: You know why your son died, don't you? Because you got involved in all this stuff. Implying that I hadn't been a good enough mother. And they used my parents to threaten me too: Remember, your parents are still alive. Threatening to kill my parents if I didn't cooperate.

One of the things you learn, and I think it was there that I first understood this—because we women never used to think of ourselves as different from the men, we were all just human beings, compañeros who were fighting together for a better, more just society. We had a common cause. We didn't distinguish between the men and the women. It was there in that torture chamber that I learned about the special treatment they reserve for women.

That whole double morality thing. Because on the one hand they said I didn't deserve to have children, that I was a bitch and they were going to sterilize me. But at the same time, individually, whenever one of them had me alone he'd try to rape me. He'd come in, put the hood on me and a rubber bag—like a tire that chokes you—and those electric shocks in my vagina. . . .

The way they approach the female body. They'd tell us we were traitors to our womanhood, as they conceived of that. How can a woman be involved in this sort of thing, they'd ask, along with men, no? Telling us that war is a man's business, or fighting against war is something for men alone to be involved in.

They can't stand it when they see a woman who thinks for herself, who wants to change the course of history, who wants to change her country's future. That was the tone when they were all torturing me together. But when each of them would come in by himself, he would tell me he wanted me to have his child. I want to have a child with you, he'd say, mocking me with that. I had to struggle, so they wouldn't be able to penetrate me. And morally speaking, they were never able to.

I think when you're being tortured, in the context of the relationship between the torturer and his victim, the person being tortured is able to maintain his or her dignity because we have a different morality. We knew why we were fighting. And the last thing any of us expected was to come out of that struggle alive.

I never thought I was going to survive. Each one of them, alone, tried to rape me. It was a terrible struggle. Space was a problem too. My feet were tied, I was forced to squat, with my hands behind me, and I was blindfolded. The only recourse I had was my voice, my words.

So when one of them would tell me: I want to have a child with you, or when I had my hands tied behind me and one of them would put his erect penis in my hands and say: look what you do to me, or when I felt a penis rubbing up against me, the only thing I could do was to say: listen, I'm not taking anything to avoid getting pregnant. If you make me pregnant, I'll bring our child right here to the DIN. I'll bring it right here and you'll have to deal with it.

What I'm saying is that I was physically overpowered by them, but not morally or emotionally or ideologically overpowered. The only recourse I had was to attack their morale, because they wanted to rape a woman who was afraid. But my words were not the words of a woman afraid. I always spoke to them directly, with as much power as I could muster. I'd tell them: If you make me pregnant, I'm not on the pill, I might very well become pregnant, and I'll come right back and deliver my baby here. That was a big help. Of course I'm not saying it wasn't rape, just because they didn't penetrate me. It was still rape, each touch, each abhorrent caress.

MARÍA: I want to say, listening to Nora now, listening to her talk about the resources she managed to use, it's the first time I'm hearing some of these things. And it's now, as Nora says, since I too have moved toward a greater consciousness of the difference in women's lives, that I fully understand how differently we were treated.

There's so much that we didn't share back then, that I'm hearing now for the first time. And I'm amazed. The similarity of how we confronted what they did to us. And I say I'm amazed because I think we women develop ways of dealing with these things from the very position of subordination in which we find ourselves.

I was treated somewhat differently. Because although I was taken into the torture chamber and although they hooked me up to the electricity, in my case they never turned it on. But when they tried to rape me I appealed to the same argument Nora used. And I was inspired by my memory of that group of prostitutes I'd seen demonstrating in front of the DIN.

My situation was somewhat different. Early on I realized or intuited that I wasn't really part of the group—that is, I was part of it and not part of it—but that I had certain recourses I'd prepared, in fact, before ever leaving Costa Rica. Because in Costa Rica we knew what working in Honduras might mean. That coming to Honduras could mean not coming back alive. Why? Because some young Costa Rican men and women had been disappeared in Honduras at the beginning of the decade.

That was one thing I had on my side, that group of Costa Ricans who had been disappeared in Honduras several years before. It was a well-known case; it had been brought before the Inter-American Human Rights Court. I had that on my mind and on my side. And then there was the attitude toward Costa Ricans that's so prevalent in Central America: that we Ticos are slightly stupid and naive, that we don't know what we're getting into. And also that we're arrogant. Because Costa Ricans are notorious for thinking they're the Swiss of Central America. And so of course I made use of those stereotypes.

For example, all the time they were interrogating me I'd say: Well you know this is a mistake, and I certainly hope it will be resolved as quickly as possible. I knew they had to be trying to find out who I was, and so I gave them the information they needed to find out, and also so they in turn would feel threatened.

I'll give you three examples. First of all, I had my Costa Rican passport, my ACNUR identification, and a card identifying me as a teacher—my ID from the university. I just kept telling them I was a teacher, what I had come to Honduras to do, and that if they wanted they could check this out at the refugee camps. I told them I'd been training literacy workers. And I said I hoped that they would rectify their mistake in having picked me up and that they would do so as quickly as possible.

I gave them the telephone numbers of my office in Costa Rica and told them to notify ACNUR that I wouldn't make it to the meeting that was taking place the following day. There was to be a meeting of the higher-ups of ACNUR. I knew about it. I didn't really have to be at that meeting, of course; I had nothing to do with the higher-ups of the organization. But I knew the meeting was taking place, and I knew they had to know this too.

The third thing I used was the fact that the president of Costa Rica's Legislative Assembly was due in Honduras to meet with government officials of that country to discuss the case of those disappeared Costa Ricans. That had become a real problem for the Honduran government, a political problem I was able to make use of by telling them they should be sure to notify their distinguished guest about the mistake they were committing with me.

I knew this because the second day at that prison I remember hearing the sound of a pair of garden shears outside a window. That's how I knew I was being held in an ordinary house that had been turned into a clandestine prison, that it had a yard and there was a gardener working outside. I recognized the sound of his shears. That gardener had a radio, and at one point he turned it on and I heard the information on a newscast.

I thought about the importance of radio, and I think of it now, fourteen years later as I work with the international women's radio program. I know how important radio can be. Among the things I heard that day on that gardener's radio was that the president of Costa Rica's Legislative Assembly was due to arrive on July 28 to the first of a series of meetings between the Costa Rican and Honduran governments, to investigate the case of the Costa Rican men and women who had been disappeared sometime before. So that was something I could use, a key element, because I knew they would have access to the same information I did.

I told them: Look, you should really get in touch with him, because at this point if ACNUR and the university find out that I didn't make it to today's meeting, tomorrow the president of our Legislative Assembly is going to be asking why not. Please explain that you were holding me by mistake, and he himself will be able to clear this whole thing up and get me out of here.

Those were my recourses, the mask of naiveté—which in fact really was naiveté in a certain sense because, contrary to what Nora felt, I always thought I was going to come out of that situation alive.

When Nora and I talked, the night before last—now that she's involved in investigating what happened and has access to some of the testimony[2]—when we talked I felt the same shudder run through my veins that I felt when I was being threatened with the torture, when they tortured me psychologically, when they threatened me with rape. The same shudder. Because now I know, for the first time, that the day before they finally freed us they were planning on assassinating us both.

What I'm saying is that the night before last was the first time I fully understood that we'd been that close to death. The mask of naiveté was very real to me at the time. It wasn't even that much of a mask. Because where violence against women is concerned, where rape or the threat of rape is concerned, what excites men, what stimulates them, is always women's fear. That and the fact that they feel they have more information than we do.

MARGARET: Okay. So now I know something about what brought the two of you to that place, to the series of clandestine prisons. Once freed, as I understand it, you had no further contact. You didn't even know one another's real names. Because the other night, when you came upon one another here, in the context of this delegation, you seemed to be seeing one another for the first time since your ordeal. Let's go back for a moment to that, to what happened when you first discovered one another here in Managua. How did you begin to speak? How did it all unfold?

MARÍA: It was right over there [she points to an adjoining sitting room, off the hotel lobby]. Nora and I actually started talking the night before last, but it was the night before that when we first saw one another, recognized one another here. The night before last, when we talked, we remembered that we did have a brief contact, here in Nicaragua, I think it was in 1987 or 1988. [To Nora] You were pregnant . . .

NORA: My last pregnancy was in 1986.

MARÍA: So it must have been 1986. Ten years ago I was coming back from El Salvador, after three years of literacy work during the war. We saw one another briefly, at a meeting we both attended. Thinking about what you said the night before last, I believe that was such a brief contact for several reasons. One, because unlike now, we weren't on an all-woman mission. There's a safety in women's space. And like you said, nothing happens by accident. In Costa Rica we have a saying that nothing happens just because. In the context of women's space there's not only safety but the possibility of a much deeper sort of exchange.

And also back then, in 1986, we were still living a situation of compartmentalization, or clandestinity if you will. What I mean is that the less you knew about someone else's life, the better. Because you were less likely to put your foot in your mouth if someone asked about that person.

I felt—and Nora, you can say whether you also felt this—particularly in a situation like that, when you recognized one another but didn't know what the other person was involved in just then, what sort of work they might be doing, that the less said the better. At the time we still felt threatened, threatened with the possibility of being picked up all over again, anywhere in Central America. So you operated under a protective guise.

You think you're protecting the other, and on some level you are. But on another level you're not protecting her at all. This is important. Because here, in the safety of this women's space, the conditions are created so that we can truly protect one another, instead of abandoning one another under the guise of that other, more limited, sort of protection.

Do you know what I mean? In a world ruled by patriarchy, we never get to hear and really support one another. It's like domestic violence. Each woman lives in her own closed environment, with no support from other women who may be going through the exact same thing, or something similar.

Nora and I came upon one another my first night here, which was October 14. We came upon one another in that room over there, where some of us who had already arrived were sitting around talking. Nora was leaving the room as I was coming in. And we looked at one another. I'm actually twenty-five pounds heavier than I was back then—plus the fact that we both lost fifteen pounds or so in the course of those ten days. Nora is also heavier.

NORA: Oh I was so thin back then . . .

MARÍA: Of course. But neither one of us even had to open our mouths or look at the other's feet. I didn't have to look at Nora's feet to recognize her here the night before last. I looked at her eyes; I saw her smile; I looked at her prominent cheekbones. Because when I saw Nora for the first time after they took our blindfolds off, that's the image I had the other night.

We hugged. We hugged. And we stayed like that, holding one another. Neither of us said a word.

MARGARET: Were you the first to recognize . . . ? Or you?

NORA: No. We both . . .

MARÍA: We just saw one another . . .

NORA: The contact was physical—on both our parts, an instantaneous physical recognition.

MARÍA: We touched in the doorway.

NORA: We touched physically and emotionally. Our sentiments spilled out, our emotions. And I want to say something here. When I'd seen María before, I'd felt that old fear. We were forced to speak about other things. We couldn't talk about our common history. Because how could I know what she was doing at that point? How could she know what I was doing? What could we have shared?

It's important to say this. Imagine what we were forced to hide. It wasn't simply what we'd been through together; it was also having to keep quiet about it. Because after we got out of prison, we each continued our work with different groups, and I for one only allowed myself very occasionally to think about what I had been through. One had to push the experience down, somewhere in one's body, accommodate it deep in a place where one could deal with it as best one could.

Imagine the conditions we were living in then. In such conditions how could we have spoken? What we needed to talk about was precisely what we'd been through together. But we didn't have the conditions for that, not then.

MARGARET: What has this meeting been like for the two of you, I mean in the sense of finally being able to open up? Has it been hard? Has it been useful? Has it been the same for both of you, or different?

MARÍA: Well, like we've said, nothing is coincidental. To tell you the truth I thought a lot about whether or not to come on this women's observer mission. Because it wasn't a great time for me to be traveling. I had a lot of work with the international feminist radio show, and I had to think twice about whether or not I should come here.

But I finally did decide to come, because every time I've been to Nicaragua, well, Nicaragua, for those of us in Central America, is a place, a context, a circumstance that always seems to bring people together. It puts us in touch with the Nicaraguan women, with ourselves, and with what we've all been through.

So I told my colleagues at work—the other women who are at the radio with me—I think I have to go, because I've always enjoyed being in the center of history. And history is going to be made there. Of course I was thinking about the history that a women's observer mission might make, not my personal history.

I said: These crazy gringas, look at the group of women they've managed to bring together! Because of course I knew a lot of the names. I was looking at the list, and I told my co-workers: the only name I don't know on this list is the woman from Honduras! I knew all the rest: Lourdes Inday from the Philippines, with whom I've worked so intensely around the issue of women's human rights and with the Comfort Women from the Second World War . . . I mean everyone. Some of the women from the United States I didn't know personally, but I knew their work, like you Margaret. But I said: This woman from Honduras . . . she's the only one I don't know.

Then, oh my God, when I got here and saw her face, I knew! I hadn't recognized the name. Nora Miselem was just a name on a list to me then. So, from the moment I arrived, and still wondering whether or not I should have made the trip, from that moment I said to myself: Shit, this is worth having come for. Here I am, and I'm not going anywhere. Because this has turned out to be an observer mission to observe the elections and also to observe myself, to be able to look at myself in this mirror which is Nora.

NORA: That's just what I wanted to say. The day after we found one another, I looked in the mirror and there you were.

MARGARET: Yes, and you know, I got a similar image the other night when Pat Humphries sang that song, the one with the line: I look into the mirror and see you. I thought of the two of you. I guess it's also not a coincidence that Pat chose to sing that particular song.

MARÍA: Look, I want to say something else. Back in Costa Rica, when I heard that in Honduras they were exploring the possibility of bringing to trial some of those responsible for the violation of human rights in the eighties, I said to my comrades in the movement, that's when I began to remember, without knowing the names . . . that is, I told one of my colleagues: I feel vindicated somehow. Because in Honduras they're beginning to reopen those cases. But I also know the sort of half-hearted results that are usual with these so-called truth commissions, with all these processes. They end up putting us back in touch with our pain, with our strength, with our history. But justice is rarely done.

And I said—at that point I didn't even remember, two nights ago Nora had to remind me of the date—because I've written about it, I have a book I've never published, with some of the events, but none of the dates, nothing precise. So when Nora told me: I'm opening my case, and we've been trying to find your name, so the investigator could locate you and you could give your testimony, right away I said: I'll be a witness, just tell me what I have to do and when. That feeling I'd had in Costa Rica, that feeling of vindication that so many of the men and women in Honduras were able to open their cases. I felt connected again. And to connect with this is to be connected with what made us act in the first place, with the struggle, the pain, the strength, all those mirrors . . .

And to reconnect in the midst of this group of women guarantees that we're not alone. This is also why this has been so important. Others of the women, that night when I told them, they said: well, this makes it worth our being here too. I'm talking about the organizers of the mission. And the very fact that you suggested doing this interview, Margaret, this strengthens the connections as well. Because now it's not just the two of us.

MARGARET: There are so many layers of meaning. I wanted to ask, Nora, how was it that you decided to open your case? I'm sure it wasn't an individual decision. And what do you expect from the process? I understand, as María just said, that the only sure thing is that you will be able to reconnect with your own history, your pain, your survival. But I wanted to ask, do you also hope for something else? Because we've seen what's happened in Argentina, in Chile, in Uruguay, where these processes have so often led to frustration.

NORA: What can I say? It's something we think about all the time. Not just the possibility that it will lead to frustration but the sense of bitterness, of impotence. When I heard that they were opening up the possibility in my country, that they'd established this ministry— which had been established constitutionally for a while but hadn't yet been organized in fact—with all its special branches: one for women, one for children, and that an important branch was the one on human rights, well, we were lucky because within that structure they named a woman who is very capable and has a real commitment to retrieving our country's history.

She is very committed, and she has surrounded herself with some young people, healthy young people, people who are conscious of the fact that we all owe society some clarification about what happened in our country. Right then, when I found out, I began calling people. In the first place, Father Fausto. I began calling everyone who had lived through, who had survived that period.

MARGARET: What's this woman's name?

NORA: Sonia Marlina Dubón. She is the Special Attorney General for Human Rights in Honduras right now. So, what happened: I began calling people. I said okay, this is our chance to bear witness, all of us, and not just to give our testimony but in some way to vindicate our ongoing desire that justice be done. So I called the other women who had been through the same experience, and we all went down together.

Each of us gave our testimony before a series of judges, but they didn't even have a proper locale for recording our stories. They listened to us in the offices of the Supreme Court of Justice, but they didn't record anything we said. Nothing. At least in my case. When we left the building there were a lot of journalists.

Later I got to thinking about it, and of course there were a great many contradictory feelings. I was confident, hopeful—and then at the same time I felt as if they'd used me for some kind of show. I asked myself, what image of Honduras is it that they want to present? I didn't want to allow myself to be used. Still, I was sure that I had to go through with it, that there are things worth fighting for, nothing happens without struggle.

I waited and waited. Until finally they developed an infrastructure for the Public Ministry. And they called me back. I went and again gave my testimony. But this time it was different. There have been different judges, not the special attorneys general but the judges who handle each case. Of course one of the limitations is that it's not just about commitment or good intentions. It's not just about knowing that you owe it to society to bring these things to light. All those people depend upon a political structure. And we know that ultimately they're not the ones who are going to decide what happens. They're the ones we have access to, with whom we can externalize our rage, our anguish. . . . And we've all heard our fill of next week . . . next week . . .

The last time around they told me I hadn't presented enough proof. I had photographs, witnesses, and one witness who could testify about what happened to me, how I looked when they released me, the marks of the handcuffs. She's a psychologist too, so she was able to testify to my emotional state at the time, when they released me from solitary confinement.

MARGARET: How long were you disappeared?

NORA: Nine days, from July 26 to August 3. In different parts of Honduras.

MARGARET: They were constantly moving you around?

NORA: Yes. Up to the last jail, which was legal. That was a relief, when we all found ourselves together in a regular prison. Because we were together and because we knew it was a legally established place. We felt stronger, more like we might get out of there alive.

At first, when they brought us to that last place I was so exhausted, so exhausted. And what I was able to see below the blindfold made me wonder if I wasn't in a cave of some sort. That was the first impression, that we were in caves carved out of rock. And I thought: well, it's all over now.

In one of the previous prisons I'd known that we were near the sea, and that was frightening too. To keep our strength up we always sang, the two of us sang as loud as we could. We didn't know, we couldn't know what was going on or where they were holding us, but we'd talk and sing. It turns out that was a recuperation prison, a place where they took prisoners they were going to release.

What was I going to say about the prison at Puerto Cortés? Ah yes, that at that moment, at the moment of being picked up, I'd been reading a book, unfortunately I can't remember the title, *Molinos de viento* (Windmills) I think it was called. I'd only gotten as far as the prologue, in which the author describes walking along a beach, sorting his ideas in order to write the book. Maybe it was *Molinos de la ira* (Windmills of rage) or something like that. I've always wanted to find that book again. Anyway, I'd just read the part where the author writes: I'm walking on the beach, I'm sorting through my thoughts for this book. . . . And suddenly he describes seeing a woman's shoe, or a child's tennis shoe, something like that. And he begins to think about the disappeared. I thought of that when I realized we were near the sea, and I thought: well, this is the end for us too. They're going to throw us into the sea.

MARGARET: Now that you mention the sea, I wonder if you would tell the story you told on the bus, about when you got your period. Because that happened there, didn't it?

MARÍA: I want to say something first, about what it was like for me to know that we were near the sea. Because I come from Puerto Rico, from a family of fishermen and fisherwomen. And when I began to smell the sea air—I didn't know where we'd been taken, and I wouldn't have known even if I'd heard a name—but when I felt the closeness of the sea, and began to hear the waves breaking against the shore, that sound of waves was comforting to me. I was exhausted, because I don't know if we mentioned how famished we were. Once a day they'd bring us half a glass of water and a tortilla, sometimes with something on it, a bit of cabbage or something. The sound of the ocean was very comforting.

NORA: At that last prison?

MARÍA: No, the one before that.

NORA: Because they never gave me anything to eat at all.

MARÍA: Yes, I know I was treated differently.

MARGARET: [to Nora] They never gave you anything to eat, in the nine days?

NORA: Right up until the end, when one of the guards decided to share his own food with me; he gave me a little bit. Right up until then. And that was the day before they let us go.

MARÍA: I drank some water and ate a tortilla, maybe once a day. But I also lost track of time, of the days and nights, of the hours. I remember

at least three tortillas during that time. And we'd been in three different prisons by then. Yes, maybe once a day or maybe once every two
days, I don't know.

The truth is, I wasn't really hungry. I'd eat when they brought me
something, because I thought: who knows, maybe this is the only
chance I'll get. So I'd eat even if I didn't feel like it. But when I heard
the waves I got a burst of energy; they revived me somehow. And at the
same time I remember thinking we actually might be in more danger
there.

My perception was that they had put us in coffins. Why? Because this
was a recuperation prison — of course we didn't know that until later —
things got better. In any case, whether or not we knew we were in a recuperation prison, I felt like they'd put us in coffins; I was sure they
were coffins. And I said to myself: shit, now they're going to toss these
coffins out to sea.

NORA: Exactly . . .

MARÍA: That's what I felt. At the same time, as I've said, I never thought
I was going to die. And I have a brother who has retrieved many things
from the ocean, things he's found floating there. So I said to myself,
maybe this will be our salvation. Maybe a boat will find us. Still, I was
sure they were coffins.

But I'll tell you why things began to get better there. This has to do
with our first verbal demand, right? We demanded that they not shut
the lids on us. And the guard began to laugh. The thing was, we weren't
in coffins. We were under some benches. Later I figured it out, because
I could see people's feet moving past. We were still blindfolded and our
hands were tied behind our backs, but I figured out that they had us
under some benches. And they seemed frightened. Maybe they knew
they were going to have to let us go.

That's when I understood that they might be about to free us, and
who knew what would happen then. They began handling us more care-
fully, and they had us under those benches so we couldn't get loose.
They sat on top of us. Those weren't coffins.

Besides our demand that they not close the lids on the coffins, the guard who was there began to talk to us. He'd answer our questions. He wasn't telling us what we wanted to hear. We weren't asking what we really wanted to know either. But he talked to us; he answered our questions. And that's when he shared his food with us. He had it in little bags, remember? And he removed the rags from our mouths.

We were together by this time. They'd covered our mouths. I remember the moment we realized we were together, and we got as close as we could so we could communicate with one another. And it was terrible for me when Nora was able to tell me what they'd done to her. That's when I realized she and I had been treated differently. We got as close as we could, because that was the only way we had of supporting one another.

And that was when Nora told us: I'm menstruating and I want a bath. And I want a sanitary napkin. We already knew that one of the guards went out to buy his food somewhere around there; we figured it was some sort of little store. That's where we prepared our first collective demand, collective and fully articulated. And we knew we were going to take it as far as we had to. I remember—with Reina too, another woman I met there—I don't remember how we decided, whether it was Nora who made the demand or all of us together. I don't remember the details, but I know that our demand was that Nora be allowed to take a bath and have a sanitary napkin.

MARGARET: Do you remember, Nora?

NORA: I think our recourse was strength in numbers. I remember saying: I want to take a bath. I didn't ask. I said it. I was asphyxiated by then, desperate. Because I could feel that hot blood. It wasn't my normal period; I was bleeding because of the electric shocks. When I said: I want to take a bath, I want to take a bath, they took me to a very uncomfortable bathroom. And the first thing I did was let the water run over me, because I felt like I was burning up.

This is a sensation that has remained with me. Especially when I read or listen to the testimonies of women who have been raped. My vagina has become a totally reflexive organ. So, what happened back there? I went to bathe, and that's when I realized where we were, I mean that we were in Puerto Cortés.

MARÍA: Do you remember how you knew? From the letters on the sign.

NORA: Yes, there was a sign, something about health.

MARÍA: Fumigation.

NORA: That's right, fumigation. It was behind the door. Or on the door. Yes. I was able to take a bath. And something else, something incredible: I don't remember what they brought me, a little towel or something; it wasn't a sanitary napkin. It was a little piece of cloth. And I remembered that Narcisa had told me: I'm bleeding too. And we managed to split that little towel in two, so we could share it.

MARÍA: Yes, but I want to say something about that, before you tell . . . Because now, from this vantage point, I understand that the dynamic doesn't only have to do with reducing women to a state of helplessness but also with trying to get us to compete with one another. I remember, for example, that when we formulated your demand—maybe you were the one who stated it, maybe it was all of us together, I can't remember—but when we told the guard, the first thing he asked us was whether the rest of us didn't want baths too. And Narcisa and I said no. What we wanted was for Nora to have a bath. Because somehow we knew, we intuited, that if we all said we wanted baths, they'd take some of us and not others. So our collective demand, without even thinking that much about it, was that we wanted Nora to have the bath.

Of course we knew that Nora was the one who had been the most severely tortured. There was no question in our minds. And we didn't get baths. We heard her bathing. When she came back, that's when she told us about the sign she'd managed to glimpse, and how she knew where we were. For me, to say Puerto Cortés was like saying Southeast Asia or wherever. What did I know, right? It was all the same to me.

What wasn't all the same was that now we had more information, we were gaining some control over our situation.

Nora came back from her bath. She had that little towel she was going to share with Narcisa. And now we knew where we were. From then on out, it was a process of gaining space. Remember? When we said we weren't going to sit down anymore, when we got them to take the rags from our mouths, and when we began to talk, to sing. Silly songs, but remember how much joy they gave us?

NORA: I remember there was a Sandinista there. I could hear him . . .

MARÍA: That's right.

NORA: Donald. He was crazy from the torture, you could tell. All he did was sing, and he'd repeat and repeat: Carlos, I'll follow you to the death.[3] The first thing I did when I got out was to call someone immediately and tell them: Go to the Nicaraguan embassy and tell them there's a Sandinista in a clandestine prison in Puerto Cortés who's been tortured, who's crazy from the torture.

MARGARET: I want to go back for a moment to the issue of menstruation, because when you first mentioned it on the bus, we talked about male fear. It's mythological, the fear men often have of women's bleeding. I remember we talked about that. I don't know if you felt that at the time, or if this is a later reflection. Because you referred to the demand as a sort of turning point, a key moment.

MARÍA: It was. About the menstruation, what was it that we intuited or felt back then? What I felt, anyway, was simply that this was something we couldn't ignore. From our own perspective. Not from the perspective of male fear. And then too, I knew, from the few things Nora had managed to tell me, that she'd been raped. So when she told me she was bleeding, that was reason enough for joy. Because it meant she wasn't pregnant. That was cause for celebration. And we celebrated by singing.

NORA: I remember.

MARÍA: Our first song was about that.

NORA: But also the anguish . . .

MARÍA: The anguish too.

NORA: But it was incredible, really, how we spontaneously and collectively knew how to proceed. I mean, maybe it did have to do with their fear of menstruation, because I remember trying to make this one guard feel as bad as I could. Around the fact that I was menstruating. Do you know what I told him—the guy who took me in to bathe? I was completely dressed, and my clothes were stained with blood. I told him: It must be from the electric shock.

He said: No, no, don't talk about that, don't tell me about that. . . . He didn't want to hear about it. But I kept on talking. And I remember going into great detail, to terrible lengths, you know, telling him things like: I must have aborted my child. I was pregnant and I must have aborted. I knew that I wasn't pregnant. I didn't even have a partner at the time. But I wanted that guard to feel some guilt for what I was going through.

And you know what they think about abortion. In their opinion, women are for having children. I wanted to make him feel as guilty as I could, to feel the horror of what they'd done to me, the horror of the torture. So I told him: I must have lost my baby. I was pregnant. To make him feel worse.

MARÍA: I do think that men's fear of women's bleeding plays a part. Because I remember—and Nora, you can say if you also remember this, because Nora is my mirror—I remember that we women sang, we celebrated, and the men, our own compañeros, were silent. What's more, one of them begged us to stop singing. He wanted us to go back to the situation we'd been in before. He was afraid that if we showed our strength like that it would go badly for all of us. Our male compañeros actually wanted us to assume a more passive stance.

So it wasn't just the situation we were in with regard to the male guards, but with our own male comrades, in terms of this thing that they weren't able to celebrate. In retrospect, I ask myself if this doesn't have to do with the fear men tend to have, the fear of menstruation. Because it was something they couldn't share, do you know what I mean?

And of course we were caring for them as well. We'd huddle together to keep one another warm, and it was all of us together, the women and the men. But the time came when we women assumed a different attitude, when we began to use our female power.

NORA: That's right. When they were torturing me in the first prison where they held us, I remember one of the things they did was to take me out and put a machete against my throat, and I remember my only fear was that they might not kill me, that they might leave me half alive. And I'd stretch out my neck and I'd tell them to do the job right, not to leave me half alive.

There were days they'd keep us I don't know how many hours; I didn't know if it was night or day, or what was true and what wasn't. They'd come; I'd hear their footsteps. They'd come to where I was, and they'd grab me and pull back the firing pin in their weapons, and pácata: they weren't loaded. No bullets.

I don't know how many times they did that. I tried all sorts of things. I tried to kill myself by hitting my head against the wall. I wanted to kill myself for the fear of what might come next. I was afraid a time might come when I wouldn't be able to stand up to them.

You know, they used this method of the good guy/bad guy. The good guy would come around and say: All you have to do is talk, just cooperate. . . . And he'd mention my parents: Salím is worried about you; Juanita is worried. And I'd think, this guy knows who I am. Then the bad guy would make his appearance. They'd switch on and off like that, trying to get us to go through different emotional states as quickly as possible. The questions . . . fast fast fast, in order to erode our morale. You had to keep alert, try to figure out what information they were really after. It was difficult to keep calm. What they wanted was for us to sink into some terrible depression, where everything becomes abstract.

And I'm telling you, when I got out of prison I spent months, months, going over and over the same things. It was like a moving picture. What did they ask me? What did I say? What did they ask me? What did I say? That was my whole world for a while. It was horrible. I couldn't stop the film. The defense mechanisms one has to develop in order to deal with this sort of situation, it doesn't make it easy to open up. It hasn't been easy.

MARGARET: I was going to ask if this interview, if talking like this, has been difficult for you. If it's made you feel bad. Or made you feel good. Or if it's been the same for both.

NORA: It's like traveling the length of one's own history, but inside. It makes one go deep inside, go back and remember. Look into those files we keep in our bodies and souls. And then bring it all up and out. To where we are now. That's the way I feel.

MARÍA: For me, well, it's a continuity, something that had to take place between the two of us. Who knew when, but it had to happen. For me, when Margaret suggested we come together and have this conversation, I didn't think twice before saying yes.

What's more, I've been working in radio for the past five years, using the radio like you use your tape recorder and like Liz uses her video camera. So I understand both sides of the question. The very experience of radio: it never occurred to me that one day I'd be the one being interviewed, even though I've interviewed so many women.

I know that our voice is also a mirror. It's not just the image; it's also the voice. And the way we work with the international feminist radio program is that when women [I am interviewing] have externalized their inner selves with me, it has also brought out my own. But this is the first time I've experienced this sort of interview, specifically set up so that Nora and I can tell our stories. And for me it's simply been a continuation of that first night, when we recognized one another, and of the conversations we've had since.

For me it's also been very important that there are other women present—you all—who are here with your microphone, your camera, your tape recorder. Because if you stop to think about it, the dynamic began with our responding to your questions; there was that sense of mediation, and then more and more we began speaking to one another. One to one.

And this is reflected in those key moments. Like when we spoke about menstruation. I think this sort of interview strengthens the connections we can make. And I want to say something else: I felt—and Nora and I talked about this the second time we spoke—I told her I'm ready to take on whatever role I need to. I'm willing to go to court, to travel to Honduras, whatever it takes. I'll make room for it, make time for it in my work plan.

And it turns out that with so many means of communication in women's hands now, we're already doing what we need to do. You, Margaret, are making it possible by stretching the space, by making our story available to more people. And you, Liz, by filming it. And I think that when this women's observer mission assesses what it accomplished, there will be things like this that nobody expected. They'll be a part of what happened here.

NORA: Wait, because I never really finished answering your question about the court case—where we are with that. You asked me what I think, what I expect from opening my case. It's incredible that we're here, together again, reliving what we experienced together back then. I've also been working in radio, with a program called "Time to Speak." Interesting, isn't it? That both of us are working in radio now. . . .

But with regard to the court case, I've given that a great deal of thought. I try to be objective, and of course that's hard. Because it's my life we're talking about. But I ask myself not only *what* I hope for but what I *can* hope for. I've told you about the people who are involved, how committed they are, how responsible—the people who work for the Public Ministry in the department of human rights.

But that's not really the point. We all know that they aren't the ones who are going to make the final decisions. In fact, I believe it's all been decided already. And we certainly aren't the ones who are going to define what we mean by justice when we ask for justice. It's the higher-ups, maybe even beyond the borders of Honduras.[4]

What gives us confidence is that we can deal with the memories now. We don't have to forget the past, that recent and painful past. Particularly now, when they're trying to get us to inhabit this thing they call the New World Order. They may think they can get us to conform by pretending that some sort of justice has been done. But if our struggle once meant life or death, if it once meant torture for so many men and women, in these new conditions what does our struggle mean? What are we fighting for today?

We're fighting for our political rights, our civil rights, our economic rights, our cultural rights. We're fighting not to be repressed. Our rights as citizens were suspended back then. That's why we had to go through what we went through. So what's the situation for us now? Our economic rights, our cultural rights are more trampled than ever. There's more misery now; life is harder. And for women, well we know that within the population as a whole, women are the poorest of the poor.

So I think this thing we call democracy is pretty restricted, it's true. But right now I have the opportunity to speak out. To tell my story. To go on television and publicly denounce what was done. To demand justice. Which brings us back to the meaning of justice. What do those of us who lived through those events expect from this opportunity to speak out?

I think all we really expect is to be able to dot the i's and cross the t's, to achieve a sort of closure to this chapter of our history. To understand what happened and why it happened. Maybe opening our cases will bring us to a place, like a retaining wall, so it can't happen again. And so that what happened won't be forgotten.

MARGARET: I'm glad you've touched on the issue of memory, of not forgetting, because there's something else that I wanted to ask each of you.

MARÍA: Before that, I want to comment on something that Nora was saying. Because your question moves us into another area, doesn't it?

What I want to say is that for me, for those of us from Central America, those of us who have lived through this sort of thing—and I feel this especially since I've been working in radio these past five years—what's important is to be able to give voice to the experience, to our own sense of it, the pain, the strength, the joy we women come away with.

For me, if I had to limit our message to just a few words, what I'd want to urge is that people don't forget that they have choices. Those choices we've given ourselves and those we've constructed with our histories. And we can't forget the choices made by those in power. Because the people with the power continue to make the same choices, now and for the future.

So every time I take on a job, do an interview, interact with someone, teach a class, especially with young people and also with some who aren't so young—because not everyone has lived these things in the same way—in every one of these contexts I think we have to continue to look at our choices. For me, in terms of what you were just saying, in terms of the burden that neoliberalism places on us, in terms of globalization, for me the Achilles heel is something we've been developing out of the women's movement, out of feminism. Because one of the things globalization tries to get us to believe is that everyone is dancing the same dance, that we're all the same. But when they push that idea, it's their dance they're talking about, globalization's dance. The dance of free markets, of the impoverishment of our peoples. And they want us to accept all that as a given.

So I think it's important, just as it was important back then: what we used to call freedom of thought. Freedom of thought is important now in that we women need to be able to think for ourselves. And we have to analyze the options we've given ourselves historically. Because the truth is, when they talk about the most minimal democratization, for example, in the different electoral processes—like the one here in Nicaragua, where we are at the moment—we need to remember our options. And in doing so, we need to go back to our roots. And roots aren't only to be retrieved. They aren't only for us to recognize ourselves and remember. They can help us provide answers as well.

And this is another reason I'm giving this testimony. I often ask myself, what's the point of talking about what we did, especially if I think about it from the viewpoint of defining what justice is. Especially now that there's so much talk about justice here in Central America. But the thing is, for us, justice passes through the process of being able to speak, being able to share, being able to recognize our shared roots, and to know that those roots are pregnant with options, options that have nothing to do with submission. This is why I continue to resist. And this is also why I'm grateful to you.

MARGARET: I had another question. It might seem somewhat off the subject or marginal to this conversation. But for me it's very much connected. I'm very interested in the issue of memory in and of itself. How memory works. I was watching you, Nora, at times in this conversation, looking for words, searching for them, or picking up on an idea and then suddenly finding that it wasn't there anymore, losing yourself, losing what you were about to say.

And so my question is: in your experience, and in the experiences of others as well—because my memory is damaged too, not from torture but from an experience of sexual abuse in my childhood, and I believe that these issues are also connected—I wonder if you might speak to the issue of memory loss in some way? Have you experienced significant memory loss? And if so, what strategies have you developed to help you heal, to help you retrieve the memory? Because our memories are so important to our sense of who we are.

NORA: For a long time, for a very long time, my memory of the events I lived through expressed itself primarily in terms of physical fear. I would sometimes get very cold, almost rigid. I'd be out in the street, for example, and I'd find myself wondering if my kidnappers and torturers were to appear again, would I recognize them? What would I do?

I'd try to prepare myself, to not be afraid, to take the offensive. But that provoked a whole other series of fears. I was always testing myself. And I was always trying to deal with these fears, here in my body.

One clear example of how the fear can manifest itself in one's body is the fact that for years I bled all the time. Even during my subsequent pregnancies, I'd bleed on and off. And recently I've thought about this, because for the past several years I've been working in the area of domestic violence, with women who have experienced not only battering but sexual violence as well.

At one point I had to do a series of interviews with victims of sexual violence in Honduras. And it was terrible having to experience once again the coldness with which forensic medicine tends to describe how the raped child died, that sort of thing. I mean, not just listening to the description of the physical death, which is bad enough, but having to remember, out of my own experience, that each aspect of that abuse involves a death of sorts. Even when you survive, it's still a kind of death. I read; I participated in the interviewing process; I listened to the stories; I saw the expressions and gestures. And I'd have to stop, because I felt like I was burning up. There are times when I feel like I'm on fire. It's unbearable.

Of course this has its positive side as well. Because I know that my ideas, my values, my sentiments, also express themselves with an almost exaggerated coherence in my physical being. This sort of thing immediately evidences itself in my body.

When the two women from South Africa read their poems the other night,[5] when they read their poems about prison, this happened to me. A few months ago, in Honduras, they opened a rehabilitation center for torture victims. That's when I had the opportunity, for the first time, of talking to people—in particular, an Argentinean woman who came to Honduras. She lives in the United States, but she comes each year to work with the Mothers of the Disappeared. And this has helped me understand how the fear has become a part of my life, a part of my physical self. It's helped me tap into it in a more positive way.

For a long time I suffered terrible pain in my body, terrible pain that I didn't know how to handle. And working with this woman has been good; she's helped me learn to deal with that. Speaking with professionals has helped, and it's also helped to be able to share with other people who have experienced what I've experienced. It's been useful to understand this other type of violence we women experience and to know that the manifestations are similar. They're different but very much the same, the sudden pain we get in our bodies . . .

MARGARET: It's true. I know, because I've talked to women who have been victims of different types of sexual abuse: incest, rape, what we call ritual abuse in the United States, the abuse that goes on in satanic cults and in some of the ultra right and racist organizations like the Ku Klux Klan or Aryan Nation. It's clear that the type of brainwashing used is similar, and that it leaves similar marks: chronic pain, memory loss, dissociation of mind and body, and certain other physical effects such as those you've been talking about, Nora.

What you say makes me think that you've been able to start bringing your mind, your emotions, and your body back together again, through some very hard work. And I think that is the only way we can heal ourselves. So we can function, so they aren't able to immobilize us.

MARÍA: For me, at this stage in my life, there are so many memories registered in my body. One way I've tried to deal with this is to listen to my body. There's a Puerto Rican woman who published an article with *Fempress* about scars, about how women's histories are registered in our scars, how each scar represents a history.[6] I read the article, which came out about a year and a half ago, and then the author came to work with us at the radio station. And I told her: it's true. But there are scars we can see—scars in the flesh, on the skin—and also scars we can't see, which are much deeper. We can only read those scars by learning to listen to our bodies.

We have to learn to read our bodies and then to trust our reactions, our impressions, our emotions. For me this has been very important, an essential recourse. I'll give you one example, just briefly. Five years ago, I was jogging around the campus of the University of Costa Rica, and a guy attacked me. His goal was rape, but he didn't succeed because I was able to defend myself, which is a whole other story. I managed to get angry before I was afraid.

I was able to defend myself, and I survived. I started looking for my attacker, using all the resources and mechanisms available to me. But I never found him, with all that the police did, going back over the scene, and so forth. Then, a year and a half later, I was at the university making some photocopies. I should mention that at the time of the attack I'd been able to see this guy's face. And there'd also been a witness, someone else who was jogging at the time.

So after looking at hundreds of photographs and not being able to identify the man, a year and a half later when I was at the university making these photocopies, I accidentally dropped some papers on the floor. And when I bent down to pick them up, someone brushed my hand. I completely lost the notion of time then, the notion of where I was; everything went black. I thought I was going to pass out.

At first I thought: maybe I forgot to eat lunch. It's already three in the afternoon, maybe I'm just hungry. I tried to steady myself, and my reaction was so intense that the guy himself asked me what was happening, if something was wrong. I looked up and saw his face. And it was him, the man who had attacked me and then gotten away.

This was an experience that taught me, beyond a doubt, that we have to learn to listen to our bodies. No excuses. No looking for other explanations. When I looked up and saw this guy's face, I understood that when he'd touched me by accident my body had recognized him fully, before I even saw who he was. Before my eyes, my conscious mind, recognized his face. Because of course I'm not made up of body alone. But the combination: it's a perfect example of what we're talking about.

Another resource that's been important to me has been that of learning to see myself reflected in other people's stories. Not only to see other women when I look in the mirror but to see myself in the mirror of the other. Whenever I interact with another woman, and particularly when I listen to another woman's story, I permit myself the luxury—because it is a marvelous luxury—of seeing myself expressed. It's not a matter of reflection but of expression, of seeing myself expressed in her words. And in her body language, her emotions.

This is another resource we can use, another way we can retrieve our collective memory: not only by listening when others tell their stories but by recognizing our own experience in those stories.

This has been very important for me with my mother. And I've had to learn to read her body because there've been times when she hasn't been able to respond to me with words. When I asked my mother what she felt when I was born, her response gave me an important clue to the psychological thread of my life, to the violence which is a product of the bipolar gender construction that society imposes on women, mothers as well as daughters.

In my family I have no memories of being threatened, in sexual terms, no physical violence. But I found the answer to those feelings I've had when I asked my mother: What did you feel when you gave birth to me? She wasn't able to answer in words, but what I read in her body told me something was there.

A year later—and sometimes one has to be patient—a year later I was able to ask her to write what she'd felt when each of her sons and daughters were born. There are six of us. And she wrote the most wonderful story. She was seventy. At the age of seventy she was able to develop a third profession as a writer, and one in which she has excelled. She began to write about herself and about us.

When she gave me what she'd written, she got in her car and drove off; she left me alone to read the piece. She didn't want to stay around to see my reaction; that's why she hadn't been able to tell me in words. And when I read what she'd written, I understood. Because she hadn't wanted to have girls, and I'd been her first girl. This was key to unraveling my own memories, of the socialization of which I was a product, that ambiguous socialization which I am able to understand from a feminist perspective today.

This is something that my sisters and other women who were raised like typical little girls in that atmosphere haven't been able to understand: the pressures a mother experiences when raising daughters, the ambivalence—which is so critical, so painful, even violent in a world in which socialization polarizes everything.

Men are such and such—they have these rights, these possibilities—and women aren't, we don't. I couldn't have held these things in my memory in the traditional sense. And I couldn't have retrieved them by myself. I had to discover them in my mother. And this sort of socialization has shaped me; this ambivalence has been very present in my body.

Once, in a kind of psychodrama, I relived the experience of my birth. And I almost died of the shock. I almost died from re-experiencing, reliving what she went through, and the role that I assumed. I had to write about this for my mother; I couldn't talk about it either. So I think the written word is also important, as a vehicle for retrieving memory, and for sharing that. It's one more way we can retrieve those scars we can't see.

NORA: I'd like to talk about something I discovered yesterday, when we began to make these associations. One of the things we've had to do in order to survive what we've been through is to make things very abstract, to abstract the experience. And that's a terrible thing, terrible. It's left me with certain areas I can't remember. And when someone pushes us to start associating, it's like you enter this place and discover an extraordinary capacity to make connections.

Sometimes I get lost. Because I try to re-create the context, and I keep trying to re-create the context and re-create it, and the story gets longer and longer, and then it's hard to come back to the particular point. But there's something I've been thinking about, something I've been analyzing from our perspective as women. Marcela Lagarde talks a lot about this.[7] It's our feeling of conditioned omnipotence. Women feel omnipotent in terms of helping others but impotent when it comes to doing anything for ourselves.

We're omnipotent when it comes to giving to others. We're always there for the other person. I remember my own mother telling me: Negrita, I'd rather see you dead . . . she said this with a great deal of love, from somewhere deep inside: I'd rather see you dead, and know where to go to mourn for you, than every time there's a battle having to go down to the morgue to see if your body is there. Still, she was always there for me, very strong.

In this context I thought about something, just yesterday. And I liked this particular discovery because—how to say this?—in the context of the Central American struggles, Honduras is such an invisible country. What is it about Honduras, I asked myself. It's that Honduras is like a woman. Honduras is the woman among the Central America nations. We've given everything: people, material resources, resources of all kinds—our emotions, our love, our passions—everything in the context of solidarity. We were there for Nicaragua. For El Salvador we were there. And because this woman called Honduras has felt herself obliged to give and give and give, to others, it has made her invisible in terms of herself, her own work.

Honduras has been omnipotent for others, and impotent for herself. And so I want to retrieve this woman as well, aside from my own extraordinary mother, I want to retrieve this woman called Honduras.

MARÍA: It's interesting, when we start talking about national identity. Because when you asked the question, I also immediately thought of something that happened to me last night. We'd been talking to Margaret in the afternoon, and to some of the other women. And, among much else, I'd said that one of the things that finding you, Nora, had done for me was to help me break down the wall of pain. But even after talking for hours, I've asked myself: When am I going to be able to cry? When? Will it be after I get home? Will it be before I leave Managua? When?

When we talk about memory, I'm not only interested in writing about it or reading about it; I want it to provoke me as well. And it's not that I think I have to cry at a particular moment. But I was thinking about this and wondering, because I know that memory demands a corporal response. If we don't cry, we'll continue to hurt.

I can recognize, I can remember, I can relive, but until I cry I won't really be able to use the experience of re-membering—reconnecting the fragmented parts of myself. Last night when the South African women read their poetry, when they shared their testimony at the cultural event we had, I was able to experience my own re-membering. Their testimony returned me to prison; it returned me to my own pain and to my strength.

I was sitting up front, and I'd gotten up and moved to the back. But then I went up front again and stayed there, right in the first row. And believe me, I couldn't even handle the tape recorder. Listening to those two women brought back memories of my own visit to South Africa in 1994, when I went to produce the live show we did there. I told the South African sisters: I cried and cried and cried and cried; I spent four days doing nothing but crying.

And I remembered that at that time I had been able to retrieve another memory from my own childhood. I come from a family in which Puerto Rico's colonization was very important, a topic about which people always spoke with a great deal of passion. My godfather—my mother's brother—I must have been five or six, and I remember I asked him: But when is Puerto Rico going to be free?

Because I listened and listened—this was at the beginning of the fifties when the whole colonial apparatus was being strengthened in Puerto Rico. One day I asked this question, and my godfather exploded. He must have been tired of me asking the same question over and over. When is Puerto Rico going to be free? What I was really asking was how, but I also wanted to know when.

He told me: Look, my child, there's a country much larger than ours, and it's called South Africa. It has millions of people. It's been struggling for its freedom forever. And it hasn't been able to achieve it, not yet. It's still got a long way to go to be free. And if that country, that's so big, with so many people and such a long struggle, hasn't been able to free itself, you better keep on waiting and do what you can. Because Puerto Rico isn't going to be free until South Africa is free. And I don't think we're going to live to see it.

He must have told me that when I was five or six years old. And I flashed on it when I went to South Africa. Sometimes you cry and you know why. But sometimes you cry and you're looking for the reason. That was a magic moment, there in South Africa, in that live broadcast with sixty-seven women, all together in a little room. And suddenly I was crying crying crying crying. Until I realized, it was that memory of my godfather's answer that was making me cry. And now we have these new connections, this new experience of being able to look in one another's mirrors and see ourselves.

MARGARET: The connections are extraordinary, and the experience of retrieving them is so important. For our collective history, and for ourselves as individuals too. As women, as people in struggle. It's interesting the things that can happen in a gathering of this sort, among women, that I'm sure wouldn't happen in another sort of gathering.

MARÍA: Yes, and I want to say something about that too. In order for these things to happen, we have to remove ourselves from those other sorts of gatherings. I say this because I insist on the importance of our giving ourselves autonomous space. Which doesn't mean isolating ourselves, doesn't mean marginalization; just the opposite. Because what you say is true. If we had been in a different context, it would have been much harder. We would have had to create the space. The space existed here because this has been a women's initiative.

MARGARET: That's right. It's a space that has another shape, another style, allows for other meanings. There's another kind of spirit here. And safety. It's very clear.

MARÍA: Nothing is coincidental.

THREE

CENTRAL AMERICA
WHERE AND WHO?

When I turned off my tape recorder that afternoon in Managua, I knew I would follow Nora's and María's stories further. I didn't yet know how, but I was sure I would find a way to return to Central America—to Honduras and Costa Rica—to ask them to go deeper into their stories, to help me understand how each had arrived at the place where disappearance momentarily took over their lives.

But first, it is important to retrieve the Central America of those years.[1]

There was a time, in the late twentieth century, when North Americans—some North Americans—knew about Central America. We knew what our government wanted us to know, or we knew what tens of thousands of refugees were telling us, or maybe both.

Those refugees—without papers, most of them, and at great personal risk—came across our southern border, fleeing economic distress and political repression that often included certain death. Because the U.S. Immigration and Naturalization Service rejected almost all of these would-be immigrants, ordinary citizens from both the United States and Canada had to step in. As in our own northern states during this country's Civil War, an underground railroad developed to help the desperate. Religious congregations, especially, offered safe passage, welcoming communities, and practical and psychological aid. Our government solidly supported the several Central American regimes then committing genocide against their own peoples. We, the

North American people, took the victims in, and many of us faced political repercussions for going against our government's policies.

There was a time, in the late twentieth century, when North Americans—some North Americans—knew about Central America. Now that knowledge has faded, replaced by the need to acquaint ourselves, however superficially, with Bosnia, Kosovo, and now Afghanistan. Memory is short in a country that trains its people to forget. To understand the story this book tells, we must speak of Central America, separate out her several countries from the indistinguishable mass that those who think about her at all conjure up when reading our major media.

Our connection was a brief moment in an otherwise isolationist panorama. People in the United States are accustomed to hearing about what happens in other parts of the world only in the context of how the events effect us: momentary sound bytes offered out of context and almost always biased by rhetoric or a failure to tell the whole story.

During that parenthesis, we heard about the powerful revolutionary movements in Guatemala, El Salvador, and Nicaragua. In the latter country, the Sandinista victory and its ensuing ten years in power provoked particularly negative coverage in our press; as the United States increased its support of the Contra war, Oliver North and Contragate brought a tortured piece of Central America into our consciousness. During the same period we gained some sense of Honduras's importance as a base from which the U.S. military was launching its covert and overt operations against those revolutionary movements.

At the end of 1989, President George Bush sent 26,000 U.S. troops to invade Panama. Panamanian President Manuel Antonio Noriega—who had once been such a friend to U.S. interests—turned himself in to the invading force. He was then brought to the United States, where he was convicted of betraying U.S. trust and imprisoned for his defiance. Thousands of Panamanians were killed in this operation, which was never referred to as a war. Panama's inter-oceanic canal would soon revert to local ownership; the hundred-year lease would end with the century, and this too made it onto our nightly news.

Costa Rica, long thought of as the Switzerland of Central America (that is, neutral, clean, civilized, and without an army), became a place where U.S. retirees could live the good life cheaply, and this fact also caught our attention. In short, during this brief hiatus, more ordinary Americans came to know where the countries of Central America were, what kinds of people live in each, and something about the always uneasy relationship between U.S. foreign policy and our close neighbors.

But like other moments of U.S. concern with different parts of the world, our interest in Central America soon waned. By 1990, Nicaragua's revolutionary experiment had been voted out of power. The wars in Guatemala and El Salvador had also given way to complex compromises between rebel and bourgeois forces. The disintegration of European socialism and the end of the cold war diminished this country's concern with revolutionary movements closer to home. Even the solidarity movements, once so active, languished.

Costa Rica, economically debilitated by globalization and its neoliberal demands, continued to attract U.S. retirees. But the news stories about that country as a haven had mostly given way to fear of diminished stability. Costa Rica and little English-speaking Belize were both promoting ecotourism, but so were many other regions of the world. By the end of the decade, Panama had reclaimed the canal accompanied by only a brief outcry of pride. More and more, the ordinary U.S. citizen thought of Central America once again as a place somewhere to our south rather than as seven distinct and distinctly unique countries.

I briefly revisit these countries here, so that readers may understand more about the diverse and complex geographical, historical, geopolitical, and cultural lands that frame Nora's and María's stories. But first a few words about how the nations of Central America, with their common roots, came to be distinct.

In 1821 the region as a whole declared its independence from Spain and a Central American Federation was established. In 1822 Guatemala was annexed by Mexico, but a year later it declared its independence from that larger neighbor to the north. The Central American Federation consisted of all six countries, but from the beginning the association was volatile for various reasons. The Mexico-Guatemala border arbitrarily cut across an ancient Mayan kingdom, and the Maya people also inhabited parts of Honduras and Belize. Guatemala has periodically tried to claim Belize as part of its territory.

Nor did what we now call Central America escape the upheavals of the independence wars at the end of the nineteenth century. In 1901 the first U.S. transnational corporation, United Fruit, arrived in Guatemala and set the economic tone for several of the Central American nations—a tone that would continue for decades.

Spain's Pedro de Alvarado, conqueror of the entire region in 1525, had claimed El Salvador as part of the captaincy-general of Guatemala. More than two centuries later, in 1786, El Salvador joined Honduras and Nicaragua as a single intendancy. The Salvadorans led Central America's first pro-independence revolt in 1811, which resulted in a declaration of independence ten years later. Periodic wars provoked shifting allegiances. El Salvador dates its national independence to 1838, but pro-Conservative interventions from Guatemala and pro-Liberal interventions from Honduras continued throughout the nineteenth century.

Forty-five years of Conservative rule in El Salvador finally provided a degree of political stability. Communal lands were privatized. Coffee became the country's dominant crop, and a coffee oligarchy consolidated itself into a group of fourteen of the country's wealthiest families, setting the stage for many of the conflicts to come.

Nicaragua is the Central American country in which we can most clearly see Spain's domination giving way to U.S. control. U.S. troops first intervened in Nicaragua as early as 1833, and they have done so dozens of times since. A major intervention in 1854 led to a U.S. mercenary, William Walker, proclaiming himself the country's president. The United States, interested in Nicaragua as the possible site for an inter-oceanic canal, recognized Walker, who reinstated slavery in the country. Eventually, however, the United States came to prefer Panama as the canal site.

The U.S. Marines began a twenty-year occupation of Nicaragua in 1921. Beginning in 1926 the country's working-class hero, Augusto César Sandino—precursor to the later Sandinistas-raised a rebel army. In 1933 that army, with internationalist aid from peoples all over the continent, succeeded in handing the marines their first Latin American defeat. But the United States supported the establishment of a National Guard, with Anastasio Somoza García at its head. Somoza murdered Sandino, installed himself as president, and the almost half-century of rule by the Somoza dynasty was begun.

Panama has similar origins. When the Spanish conquistador Vasco Núñez de Balboa crossed the isthmus of Panama and claimed the Pacific Ocean basin for the Spanish Crown in 1513, the country's future as a crossroads of world trade was established. In Panama, with its geographically important land strip, as in other Central American countries, England vied with Spain for control throughout the sixteenth and seventeenth centuries. Panama finally declared its independence in 1821 and joined Simón Bolívar's Great Colombia. The U.S. gold rush of 1849 also cast Panama as a valuable transit route from the Atlantic seaboard to California.

As the nineteenth century unfolded, the United States invaded Panama every now and then to protect its growing interests, and in 1902 the U.S. Congress authorized President Theodore Roosevelt to acquire a strip of Panamanian land from Colombia in order to build the coveted canal. Thus continued a history of foreign forces buying and selling Panamanian territory. The twentieth century witnessed a repetition of the same, with the United States making use of more sophisticated measures and installing local authorities believed to be supportive of U.S. interests.

In 1946 the United States opened the infamous School of the Americas, which has trained generations of local law enforcement personnel in the counterinsurgency methods they would use against their own peoples. In 1964 Panamanian students were attacked by U.S. police after demanding that the flags of both countries be flown at a Canal Zone high school. In the ensuing conflict, twenty-one Panamanians were killed, more than four hundred wounded, and over five hundred arrested. Diplomatic relations between the two countries were briefly severed, and the Organization of American States was called in to mediate.

In the late 1960s a lieutenant colonel by the name of Omar Torrijos staged a coup and consolidated power. Torrijos would be supportive of anti-U.S. movements in the region before dying in a mysterious plane crash.

In what is now Belize, the Mayan people resisted Spanish incursion as early as 1508. The British established their first settlement there in the middle of the seventeenth century, and Belize has been officially English-speaking ever since. With a population of Africans descended from slaves and many Miskito and other Indian peoples as well, it shares a cultural identity with the Atlantic coast of Nicaragua. Throughout the eighteenth and early nineteenth centuries, England and Spain fought over Belize. Slaves also staged a number of fierce revolts.

When the Central American Federation disintegrated in 1859, Guatemala claimed to have inherited from Spain a sovereign right to Belize. The laws of England were imposed, however; Spain apparently had richer lands for which to fight, and Guatemala agreed to relinquish its claim. In 1862 Belize was declared part of the British Commonwealth, under the name of British Honduras. Little Belize was important mostly for land transport; it provided a road to the coast useful both to Guatemala and the United States. This road and a series of hurricanes have shaped the country's political and economic history.

In 1945 Guatemala named Belize its twenty-third department (state). In 1961 Belize rejected another offer to become part of Guatemala and that same year obtained associate member status in the United Nations Economic Commission for Latin America. In the 1970s Belize launched both legal and military maneuvers aimed at securing national independence. The United States favored Guatemala in these disputes. In 1975 the United Nations was the scene of a first series of votes on Belize's right to self-determination. The United States always abstained.

By 1981 Belize had become a fully independent member of the British Commonwealth of Nations, and the country joined the United Nations and the Movement of Non-Aligned Nations.

During the region's declaration of independence from Spain, Costa Rica followed a path similar to those of her neighbors. Like Guatemala, it was annexed to Mexico for a time. In 1826 a civil war broke out. San José was declared the country's capital in 1835, and three years later the Central American Federation broke into five different states.

The twentieth century saw a series of elections and coups in Costa Rica. Massive strikes by banana workers were important during the 1930s. The Communist Party eventually became the Popular Vanguard Party in 1943. Five years later civil war broke out. President José Figueres (1970–1974) received substantial support from the United States, and later he admitted to having connections to the CIA.

By the 1970s, however, Costa Rica was among the few Latin American countries to defy U.S. orders and maintain a degree of trade relations with Cuba. It also reestablished consular relations with that increasingly isolated Caribbean country. In 1979 Costa Rica declared its support for Nicaragua's FSLN. Costa Rica was an important base of rearguard support for the Sandinistas, and much later it also proved important in forming the Contadora Group to negotiate Central American peace.

Contadora's other members were El Salvador, Guatemala, Honduras, and Nicaragua. In 1987 Costa Rican President Oscar Arias took a leadership role in regional peace initiatives, and the Esquipulas II Peace Accords were signed that year. Arias himself was awarded the Nobel Prize for Peace.

But Costa Rica's role as an impartial mediator has shown notable cracks. Arias allowed the United States the use of its territory to channel humanitarian aid to the Nicaraguan Contras, and more than half of the 170 Peace Corps volunteers in the country signed a petition claiming that a dramatic increase in their ranks was unnecessary and politically motivated. By the mid-1990s, the more moderate José María Figueres (son of the former president) was elected to the presidency, and the country's legislature accepted the imposition of structural adjustment. The peaceful nation that had resisted establishing an army (although its police force does much the same work), that was on the front lines of women's equality, and that had become such a haven for U.S. retirees has now been brought into the circle of U.S. control.

In 1502 Honduras, so important to our story, was the scene of Christopher Colombus's first landing on the Latin American mainland. It too declared its independence from Spain as part of the 1821 Central American Federation. In 1839 the country became an independent republic. As elsewhere, however, U.S. troops landed in Honduras in 1896. Three years later the country's first banana concession was granted to what would become Standard Fruit. United Fruit became involved in 1912.

Honduras's disputes with neighboring countries, as well as the devastating hurricanes that ravaged its land, would mark it throughout the twentieth century. The four-day Soccer War with El Salvador in 1969 flared over the mistreatment of Salvadorans in Honduras. The treaty that officially ended that war would not be signed until 1980. After the 1979 Sandinista takeover in Nicaragua, President Jimmy Carter strengthened U.S. ties to the country, and John Dimitri Negroponte became U.S. ambassador to Honduras.

Negroponte would be vital to the covert U.S. military operations that used Honduran territory as a beachhead from which to attack and subvert the liberation struggles of Nicaragua, El Salvador, and Guatemala. In November 1982, *Newsweek* revealed Negroponte as the person in control of the Contra operations against Nicaragua. Negroponte resurfaced in 2000 as President George W. Bush's appointee to represent the United States in the United Nations.

Despite their government's right-wing positions, however, the Honduran people, as Nora Miselem so eloquently tells us, have a long history of generous solidarity with their neighbors. So much so that their own liberation struggle may have suffered as a result. The U.S. military has been a major employer in Honduras, where several large U.S. bases provide jobs to a painfully unemployed and underemployed population. This economic reality too has put a damper on the development of a viable liberation movement.

Although the number of Hondurans disappeared and murdered has been nowhere near the number documented in neighboring Guatemala and El Salvador—or even in Nicaragua during the Contra war—instances of extreme atrocities are known. Nora's and María's experiences are two of these. In January 1994, human rights ombuds-man Leo Valladares issued a report on the fate of 184 people disap-peared in Honduras between 1979 and 1990. Only five survived, two of them the protagonists of our story.

GUATEMALA

Guatemala is one of the most beautiful places in the world. It has var-ied terrain—twenty-three dramatic volcanic peaks (many of them ac-tive), black sand beaches and fertile plains, jungles in which ruins of the great Mayan civilization still wait to be fully unearthed, highland villages, and pristine lakes—and it enjoys an almost perfect climate year-round.

Like much of the rest of the isthmus, Guatemala is geologically un-stable; the old capital of Antigua and the country's current capital, Gua-temala City, have been damaged by major earthquakes at least fifteen times since the sixteenth century. The old capital remains a delightful colonial retreat, where Spanish-language schools and New Age restau-rants line cobbled streets alongside graceful stone arches and Indian women selling richly embroidered cloth. The current capital is cosmo-politan and sophisticated as well as impoverished and desperate. Its San Carlos University, founded in 1676, is the oldest in the Americas. Sixty percent of the country's inhabitants are indigenous peoples, most of them Quiché.

Guatemala has been ravished by decades of war, and many of its rural villages have been scorched and razed by counterinsurgency methods reminiscent of U.S. warfare in Vietnam. Since 1980, Guate-mala's genocidal war (called The Violence by natives) has resulted in 100,000 civilian deaths, 40,000 disappeared, 440 villages destroyed, 250,000 orphans, more than 100,000 refugees, and as many as a mil-lion internally displaced persons. Guatemala's repressive regimes took no prisoners; dissidence inevitably meant disappearance, torture, mu-tilation during interrogation, and death.

Repression was continuous, brutal, and could invariably be traced to the succession of dictatorial administrations fully supported by U.S.

foreign policy. The United States government provided substantial funding, weaponry, training for local personnel, and direct involvement through advisors who oversaw and/or carried out interrogations, torture, and the physical elimination of those considered subversive.

The northernmost Central American country, Guatemala is also the most populated; its inhabitants currently total twelve million. The country was once eminently rural, but in recent years more than half its inhabitants have migrated to the cities—pushed by an imbalance in the distribution of wealth and the economic infrastructure, hunger, and government repression. The population is young, with almost half under the age of fifteen. This figure is partially the result of the fact that the average life span has been shortened by poverty and disease, and partially the result of the great numbers of people massacred through years of brutal war.

Although it is still breathtaking, in recent years Guatemala's great beauty has suffered from some environmental deterioration. This can be seen in damage to the country's impressive landscape as well as in its weary land base. Skewed land-tenure patterns, military dominance, the absence of a well-developed civil society, and the repression of workers and peasants have stalled the country's political and economic development.

Guatemala is a land of contrasts. Tourists enjoy Antigua with its colonial beauty and charm, while highland laborers pick coffee for a dollar or two a day. The mystery of the ancient ruins of Tikal and the intricate beauty of contemporary Mayan art (the country's rich fabrics are exquisite) coexist with the army's campaigns of psychological terror. Fundamentalist Christianity has made great claims on the hearts and minds of a people who once practiced Catholicism interwoven with Mayan ritual; Pentecostal preachers have now saved the souls of close to half the country's poor.

For the purposes of this brief overview, we can date the country's modern history from 1944, when longtime dictator Gen. Jorge Ubico retired and the regime that succeeded him was overthrown by a reformist alliance of military officers, students, professionals, businessmen, and politicians. For the next ten years, Guatemala experimented with democracy. There were social reforms, and broader sectors of society began to have access to the economy and a certain degree of modernization. But in 1954, as so often happens when one of the United States's client states makes a bid for independence, the CIA supported a violent coup. The era of reform was over, and the next four decades witnessed a continuous litany of horror.

A strong guerrilla movement—led by the country's official Communist Party (PGT), the Guatemalan Army of the Poor (EGP), and the Guatemalan National Revolutionary Unity (URNG)—emerged to fight this horror on several fronts. Eventually it succeeded in forcing the government to the negotiating table. A Quiché Indian woman named Rigoberta Menchú, whose martyred father had been a peasant leader and whose family continued to endure brutal repression, brought the plight of Guatemala to the attention of the world in her book *I, Rigoberta Menchú*. She was awarded the Nobel Peace Prize in 1992.

Another woman, this one a North American attorney named Jennifer Harbury, made the world aware of U.S. complicity with Guatemala's repressive politics. Her husband, an Indian guerrilla commander, was tortured to death by a CIA operative, and Harbury's unwavering investigation forced the U.S. government to declassify documents that revealed its direct involvement.

Today Guatemala continues to be torn by its legacy of decades of military control, racism (the minority ladinos, peoples of Spanish or mixed ancestry, still hold absolute power over the Mayan majority), a sinister shadow of state-imposed terrorism, neoliberalism's structural adjustment programs, endemic poverty and disease, and an unusually reactionary economic elite. Inflation is high and rising. The country's external debt is low when compared with that of other Central American countries such as Costa Rica and Panama, yet debt drain is hard on already meager public revenues. Public education, health, and housing standards are abysmal for the country's majority poor.

Since the end of the decades of war, there has been a notable sense of relief—an overlay of social relaxation imbued with the vivid memory of everyday terror. To the casual visitor, the country is safe and inviting. But almost everyone has a story.

Guatemala's adoption of the General Agreement on Tariffs and Trade (GATT) in 1991 marked the country's rollover into full trade liberalization. It also has free-trade agreements with Mexico and the other Central American nations. Liberalized trade focuses mainly on export production. Although this policy may broaden economic horizons for Guatemala's upper classes, and there is always a little that trickles down, the formula excludes the majority of the population.

Poverty is so widespread and dramatic in Guatemala that the statistics, horrifying as they are, really don't convey the human face of deprivation. Tom Barry, in *Inside Guatemala*, writes: "More revealing than numbers and percentages are scenes from daily life—images of how the vast majority of Guatemalan people live: the Indian woman who walks barefoot to the town market from her mountain village, carrying her sandals until she reaches town so as not to wear them out; the hundreds of thousands of Guatemalans who can no longer afford to eat beans with their tortillas; the peasant women who labor more than five hours every day (including gathering loads of firewood to cook the maize) to make their own tortillas in order to save the one or two quetzals it would cost to buy them at the local tortillería; the misery of urban squatters, living in makeshift shelters without water, sanitary facilities, or electricity." [2]

Poverty in Guatemala is defined by two categories: those without the ability to meet basic material and food requirements are said to be living below the poverty line, and those who go hungry every day of their lives are classified as living in extreme poverty. According to the country's own National Statistics Institute, 59 percent of all Guatemalans and 71 percent of rural residents endured extreme poverty in 1989. The United Nations Children's Fund (UNICEF) considers 86 percent of Guatemalans to be impoverished.

Guatemalan women exhibit an inspiring strength—witness Rigoberta Menchú and many like her—but they are less organized around specific women's issues than are their other Central American sisters. There is no large, visible feminist or lesbian movement in Guatemala City, like those in Managua, San José, or even San Salvador. There has been some very successful organizing against domestic violence, however. A movement to secure minimal rights for domestic servants (most of whom are female and routinely subjected to an almost feudal system of semi-ownership) has also been important.

An organization of Families of the Disappeared continues to demand accountability for past atrocities, and like its counterparts in other Central and Latin American countries, it is run by women. Because of the country's overwhelming history of repression, this organization represents great segments of the Guatemalan population. The liberation theology branch of Guatemala's Catholic Church has also been active in ongoing human rights work, and religious sisters as well as laywomen play an important role.

EL SALVADOR

Just south of Guatemala and west of Honduras, El Salvador is likely more familiar to the average North American than some of the other countries of the isthmus. It is the smallest and most densely populated Central American country, about the size of Massachusetts, with five million inhabitants. El Salvador's recent history has been such that news of its most dramatic moments has followed tens of thousands of refugees to the United States.

These moments belong to the long war of resistance that has been fought against a series of repressive governments. They include the 1975 murder of poet Roque Dalton by members of his own revolutionary organization, the 1980 murder of Monsignor Oscar Arnulfo Romero, the rape and murder of four U.S. church women that same year, the deaths of four Dutch journalists in 1982, and the 1989 death squad murder of six Jesuit priests and the two women who worked for them. It is estimated that 80,000 people died during the last few decades of El Salvador's long history of genocide.

These more recent deaths continue an older history. In 1931, El Salvador's minister of war, Gen. Maximiliano Hernández Martínez, led a successful coup against the country's first democratically elected president, Arturo Araujo. Hernández Martínez, a man consumed by a strange mysticism, kept bottles of blue water to ward off evil spirits and believed the killing of insects to be a sin—yet he reveled in the killing of human beings.

Roque Dalton left us a short poem about Hernández Martínez: "They say he was a good president / because he built cheap houses / for the Salvadorans who were left." Dalton was referring to the dictator's 1932 put-down of a Communist-led rebellion of peasants and workers. Thirty thousand were massacred in what has come to be known simply as *la matanza*. Hernández Martínez remained in power until 1944, the same year Ubico was overthrown in Guatemala.

Unlike much of the rest of Central America, with its dense jungles and mountainous terrain, El Salvador has few mountains or jungles in which guerrilla fighters can hide. The struggles of its people have had to be waged mostly through urban warfare in the cities. The National Revolutionary Movement (MNR) was founded in 1965, and the end of that decade and the first half of the next saw the formation of other rebel organizations, among them the Democratic Nationalist Union (UNO and UDN), the People's Revolutionary Army (ERP), and the Armed Forces of National Resistance (FARN). In 1980 these organizations came together in the Farabundo Martí National Liberation Front (FMLN), which linked the diverse armed movements and was named after a leader of the 1932 rebellion, and in the Democratic Revolutionary Front (FDR), which coordinated the civilian opposition.

Women played a particularly visible role in the struggle against El Salvador's repressive regimes. Some of the armed struggle organizations actually instituted quotas requiring that a quarter of their military and political leadership cadre be female. El Salvador is the only Central American country in which this was the case. Several well-known revolutionary leaders were women, including the FMLN's second in command. In a country in which women are more poorly educated and earn substantially less than men, and are routinely victimized by poverty and domestic abuse, Las Dignas (literally, Women of Dignity) is an organization that continues to fight for women's rights.

María, one of the women who tells her story in this book, spent three years teaching literacy on the front lines of the Salvadoran war.

Not surprisingly and despite how important that participation was for her, she speaks of a deeply embedded double standard even among revolutionaries for whom gender equality was such a loudly proclaimed objective.

NICARAGUA

Nicaraguans may be the most fiercely nationalist people in Central America. Situated south of Honduras and north of Costa Rica, this second largest of the region's countries has a population of four million. Although there is a distinct separation between the Black, Creole, Miskito, Sumo, and Rama peoples of the Atlantic coast and the mestizo majority that inhabits the much more densely populated western region of the country, all Nicaraguans revere poetry (many are poets) and carry in their blood the collective memory of repeated U.S. invasions and domination.

I've mentioned William Walker, the U.S. mercenary who was named president of the country and enjoyed a brief tenure in that office in the 1850s, as well as Augusto César Sandino (who Nicaraguans claim as their hero regardless of their political position, in the same way that all Cubans claim José Martí). I've referred to the long Somoza family dictatorship and the Sandinista rebels (FSLN) who succeeded in ousting it in 1979. Rubén Darío is another important name; he was the modernist poet (1867–1916) whose work put little Nicaragua on the international cultural map. More recent poets—Ernesto Cardenal, José Coronel Urtecho, and Gioconda Belli—painters, and musicians have, at least in some circles, made Nicaragua a household word.

The Sandinistas of the 1980s drew deeply on both their nationalism and their culture. After almost half a century of a dictatorship that shot young people for the simple crime of being young, the sense of freedom and creative possibility was everywhere. I was privileged to know some of the Sandinistas during their pre-victory years in Cuba (where I was living at the time), and soon after their 1979 win I accepted an invitation from my old friend Ernesto Cardenal, then minister of culture in the new Nicaragua, to come and research a book about women. That led to my eventually moving to Nicaragua, where I lived for almost four years.

The Sandinistas were creative in their efforts to eradicate poverty and curable disease, promote literacy and public education, make health care available to everyone, build much-needed housing, and create jobs. Many extraordinary projects were begun, and some bore fruit. Women were euphoric. Many pointed out that after fighting alongside their men, they weren't likely to retreat into the purely domestic sphere just because the war was over. But although they were resistant to reassuming traditional roles, many of them were forced to do so. The FSLN was neither able nor willing to make the systemic changes necessary for changing women's lives.

From the beginning, the United States was intent on destroying the Sandinista experiment. Presidents Reagan and then Bush were not going to permit another Cuba in the Americas.

And so the 1980s saw a struggle for a nation's soul. Guerrillas-turned-peacetime-political-leaders looked for ideas to their own Sandino, Cuba, social democracy, and Catholic liberation theology (as expressed in hundreds of base communities throughout the country). The United States funded, trained, and supported Nicaragua's disaffected, who became the fragmented but nonetheless power-hungry Contras.

About halfway through the Sandinista decade, internal conflict and corruption began to cut away at the general population's identification with the FSLN. The governing party made some serious mistakes in its approach to the indigenous peoples of the Atlantic coast. A U.S. economic embargo hurt an already fragile economy. And too many families were losing their sons to a war that had no end in sight. A center-right coalition of opposition parties, with the widow of a well-known martyr as its presidential candidate, promised that its close ties to the United States would bring desperately needed investment and put an end to the war. In 1990, with significant U.S. complicity, the Sandinistas were defeated at the polls.

This defeat coincided with the defeat of socialist, communist, and peoples' governments around the world, the end of the cold war era, and the emergence of the United States as unchallenged world power. Since that center-right coalition's tenure in office, Nicaragua has moved even further to the right. Arnoldo Alemán, an ex-mayor of Managua described by many as worse than Somoza, became president in 1996. Sadder still, Daniel Ortega, who had twice been president under the Sandinistas, ended up pacting with Alemán—and later attempting reconciliation with Somoza forces. In the 2001 elections, Ortega lost for the third time, to Alemán vice president Enrique Bolaños.

One interesting sidebar to current Nicaraguan political life is that in March 1998, Daniel Ortega's stepdaughter, Zoilamérica Narváez, accused him of having sexually abused her over a period of nineteen years. This revelation was but the tip of the iceberg; many strong Nicaraguan women have since come out against men who had in one way or another attacked their integrity or otherwise held them back. Even in the high ranks of the FSLN, the phenomenon was evident. A party that had quite literally given women voice and agency had also let many of them down.

Ortega has denied having sexually abused his stepdaughter, but Zoilamérica's testimony is powerfully credible. Ortega, as a member of the legislative body, enjoyed parliamentary immunity, and in Nicaragua a sold-out system of justice at first prevented Narváez from taking him to court. The Inter-American Human Rights Court in Washington, D.C., after considering her evidence for more than a year, agreed to hear the case. Then, after the 2001 elections, Ortega himself suddenly petitioned a local court to hear the case so, as he said, the problem could be put to rest. It took less than two weeks for the judge to rule that the statute of limitations had expired and to throw the case out. (Later the press reported that Ortega had entertained this judge a week earlier, at a party in his home.) The case before the Inter-American Human Rights Court is pending. Inside Nicaragua, Narváez has the support of many, although discussion of her case is taboo within the FSLN itself.

Corrupt forces govern Nicaragua today and likely will continue to do so for the predictable future. But the liberating experience of honest and innovative Sandinismo has not been lost. If nothing else, the FSLN

win in 1979 broke through the numbing effect of generations of political manipulation. People's creativity soared. Real change was possible.

A strong, independent women's movement is also changing the face
of this Central American country. There are now a number of women-
run nongovernmental organizations and other institutions doing the
work that was disrupted when the Sandinistas lost power. This work
includes not only gender-specific issues but concerns related to education, public health, AIDS outreach and advocacy, and youth.

PANAMA

Panama, the southernmost country in Central America, frequently is
not considered a true part of the isthmus. Panama stands alone in
many ways. On the one hand it has never been a member of the Central American Common Market, a body important in the region's economic life. On the other, despite having once been a province of
Colombia, it is rarely considered a South American nation.

What Panama shares most profoundly with its Central American
neighbors is its history of military intervention by the United States
and the ways in which its economy has been affected by United Fruit
and similar transnationals. What sets it apart—and has made it even
more dependent, sometimes seeming to be almost a U.S. protector-
ate—has been the hundred-year U.S. ownership of its canal and the
free-trade zone in Colón.

About the size of South Carolina and with three million people,
Panama is a nation of dramatic contrasts—from the modern infrastructure of the canal and environs to the nearby slums. When compared with other countries of the region, Panama has a high per capita
income. The literacy rate is 90 percent, and 83 percent of the population have access to potable water. About half the country's people live
in the Panama City–Colón corridor that borders the canal. The other
half inhabit rural towns and villages, in a world apart from their urban
neighbors.

Panamanians identify with the United States, emulate its lifestyle,
and value its commodities, while harboring a fierce resentment of U.S.

domination, particularly with regard to the canal. Anti–United States sentiment swells and bursts from time to time, whereas after the December 1989 invasion, many in the middle class were out in the streets waving U.S. flags.

Throughout the 1990s, Panama followed the other countries in the region toward demilitarization and consolidation of political democracy. Regaining control over the canal in 1999 was important for Panama's self-image, not to mention its economy. Although it remains defined by its position as an international crossroads, it has also become increasingly identified with Central America, with whose countries it shares many problems.

Because of Panama's position as a nexus of world trade and finance, the country has comparatively well-developed systems of public service, including health and education. In Central America, only Costa Rica has done better in these areas. The structural adjustments required by globalization affect Panama, but not as much as they affect its neighbors.

During the early and mid-1980s, U.S. government concern in the region was directed at Nicaragua, El Salvador, and Guatemala. As for Panama, the United States simply wanted to maintain the status quo, a status quo that had allowed military bases in Panama to serve U.S. interests for so long. The School of the Americas and other installations were important for carrying out U.S. policy. Panama's 1984 elections, fraudulent at every level, were warmly praised by Washington.

By 1987, however, Washington had reversed its position on Panama and set out to topple its president. The disintegration of the socialist bloc as well as a new focus on the drug war at home pushed the first President Bush into this foreign policy shift. The United States tried all sorts of strategies for getting rid of Noriega: economic sanctions, aid to the political opposition, and diplomatic isolation, among others. When none of these worked, Bush launched the full-scale military invasion that ended with Noriega being brought to this country to stand trial (and eventually to serve time in prison). The invasion also put Panama on the list of Latin American countries with unsolved cases of disappeared persons.

Interestingly, this heavy-handed militarism played a key role in reducing Panama's own dependence on military rule. In 1984 the School of the Americas closed after training nearly 45,000 Latin American officers; it relocated to Ft. Benning, Georgia, where thousands of protestors stage yearly and ever-larger demonstrations in an effort to close it once again. In the 1994 Panamanian elections, civilian candidates—among them a woman and a salsa star—ran to fill the vacancy left by Noriega.

Today Panama continues to play an important role in the drug trade, money laundering, and less obviously illegal forms of international commerce. The end of the last century saw the withdrawal of all U.S. troops stationed there to protect the canal. The Panamanians manage and protect their own inter-oceanic gateway now, and a new national pride accompanies what undoubtedly must be homegrown variants of the same old problems. Panama's cities continue to be as modern as cities anywhere, whereas her villages evidence a simpler, sparser way of life. Small farmers are often mestizos, and several indigenous tribes exist in the country. The Ngobe-Buglé live in western Panama, the Kuna mainly on the San Blas Islands off the country's northeastern coast, the Emberá and Wounaan in the river basin lowlands along both coasts, and small numbers of Teribe and Bokota inhabit the mountainous regions.

Panamanian women have an impressive history. One of the first all-women political parties in Latin America was Panama's Feminist National Party (PNF), founded in 1923. The PNF led the struggle for women's suffrage in the country and pushed for other social reforms benefiting women and children. Eventually, however, PNF members became targets of extreme repression. For example, all party members who were university professors lost their jobs in 1938. In 1944, many former PNF members founded the National Women's Union. Panama's 1946 constitution finally gave women the vote.

Panamanian women are well educated and well integrated into the workforce, but as in almost all other countries, as workers they suffer from wage discrimination as well as discrimination based on their reproductive status. Equality in divorce settlements and an awareness of domestic abuse and sexual harassment all draw public attention in Panama, and a new Family Code, in effect since 1994, has improved women's legal status. Women have run for president and served in the Legislative Assembly (a woman has been its president); a few are mayors.

BELIZE

Belize is a country that likely does not come immediately to mind when one thinks of Central America. To begin with, English, not Spanish, is the official language. Spanish has become more commonplace, however, and currently almost half the population considers it their mother tongue. Still, there remains a veiled stigma associated with all things latino; the people of Belize tend to equate Central American culture with marginality, even criminality. They see themselves as Caribbean, and superior. The nation's culture is in fact closer to that of some of the Caribbean islands than it is to the rest of the isthmus.

Belize is tucked up into the extreme northeast corner of Central America. It is divided from Mexico by the Río Hondo and shares a long western border with Guatemala, which over the years has made frequent claims on Belize's territorial integrity. Known until 1973 as British Honduras, Belize's 8,886 square miles (about the size of New Hampshire) remained a British colony until its relatively recent independence in 1981. Among Central American nations, only El Salvador's land mass is smaller, but with barely one-quarter of a million inhabitants to El Salvador's five million, Belize is the least populated and most truly wild.

Only 174 miles long and 78 miles wide, at its longest and widest, Belize offers a beautifully diverse topography. In the north, low plains of mangrove swamps are fed by rivers that originate on the western plateau and run to the Caribbean. One of these, the Macal, plunges one thousand feet at Hidden Valley Falls, in an area that is a remnant of the oldest land surface on the isthmus. The Maya mountains of the south include Victoria Peak (3,699 feet high) and overlook a narrow coastal strip with lovely beaches. But it is the spectacular barrier coral reef, ten to twenty miles offshore, that protects some 175 tiny islands and is the country's main attraction for an ever-increasing influx of tourists.

Wild animals now lost to civilization in most of the other Central American countries still inhabit the dense forests of Belize, making the country a refuge for jaguar, tapir, crocodiles, and many exotic birds. Even Belize's cities—a few modern buildings standing out among clumps of wooden houses reminiscent of the Atlantic coast of Nicaragua—are haphazard and erratic. Unruly traffic crowds the few paved streets (the country does not have a single traffic light), and traffic accidents constitute one of the leading causes of death.

Belize City is definitely the country's economic and population hub, although the capital was moved inland to Belmopan fifty miles to the west. This move was the result of Hurricane Hattie in 1973; because of its location, Belize has suffered many devastating storms over the years. In 1990 Belize City finally completed its sewer system, thereby tempering the stench of open canals. In 1994 the World Bank provided a $25 million loan, which is being used to improve both infrastructure and the look of the capital.

Like a number of other very small nations, Belize has managed to preserve a relatively peaceful domestic situation. There are none of the painful disputes or brutal struggles so common among the other Central American countries, none of the guerrilla wars, urban or rural. There is little crime, little visible poverty. Yet Belize lacks, among other twenty-first century technologies, the capacity to diagnose cancer or to treat it with chemotherapy or radiation. A citizen who falls ill with such a disease must travel for treatment, if she has the money. A citizen without money—like so many throughout the world—will simply die.

The people of Belize have descended from Mayan Indians, Garífuna (or Black Caribs), Africans who were brought over as slaves, Spanish-speaking mestizo immigrants from Mexico and other parts of Central America, East Indians, Middle Eastern immigrants, and a small number of Caucasians from farther north or east. By the late seventeenth century, pirates, English loggers (called Baymen), Spaniards, and kidnapped Africans had joined the native indigenous groups to begin to form what is today a powerfully beautiful racial and cultural mix.

The English established colonial control, eventually permitting a semi-autonomous political model. The People's Unity Party (PUP) is primarily social democratic, although anticommunist and—at best—ambivalent about U.S. influence in the region.

After independence, the PUP made George Price the country's first prime minister. He has advocated for what he calls wise capitalism. Later the growth of the United Democratic Party (UDP) provided some competition and rounded out a conventional two-party system. There have been smaller political configurations, Left as well as Right, but none of much importance.

So Belize remains a stalwart of internal peace, with a foreign policy largely dictated by its ties to Britain and the United States. It flaunts a degree of formal independence through membership in the Movement of Non-Aligned Nations and its long recognition of such groups as the Palestine Liberation Organization. The country has remained somewhat removed from Central American politics, preferring to think of itself as the Caribbean Beat in the Heart of Central America (the slogan of its only radio station).

Internally, although extreme poverty and people's movements for social change are not obvious, there is a high unemployment rate (18 percent, according to some sources). Only 11 percent of the workforce is unionized. Family and religion are important, and the latter is actively involved in community control.

Religion (mainly Roman Catholicism) also figures prominently in the history of women's organizations in Belize. Traditionally, these organizations have often been linked to civic action and charity work rather than women-oriented advocacy or service. As in many other third world countries, the United Nations' proclaiming of 1975–1985 as the International Decade of Women did much to bring attention to women's issues.

Today there are a number of organizations concerned with women's rights and needs, focusing on such issues as development, skills training, the special problems faced by rural women, workplace equality and salary equity, women's wellness and self-help, family planning, violence against women, and even women's creativity and art. There is some government involvement, but private nongovernmental organizations are particularly important.

Leaders of Belize's women's organizations complain of widespread job discrimination and unequal pay for women, who are often heads of families and single parents. Belize has spawned a growing garment industry in which almost all the workers are female and sweatshop conditions prevail. Within the global panorama of overseas sweatshops and maquilas, large numbers of Belize's women work in subhuman conditions and earn little more than a dollar an hour. In 1991 this situation initiated the formation of the Women Workers Union.

COSTA RICA

Costa Rica, the longtime home of one of our protagonists, with its reputation for neutrality among Central American nations, conjures up images of a tranquil landscape dotted with neat farms and picture-perfect cows, clean, safe cities, and a friendly peace-loving population. All this is true. But it is not the whole truth. A growing tourist industry, now linked to environmental concerns and ecoindustry, advertises thrilling scenes of erupting volcanoes, walks through the luxuriant treetops of cloud forests, and beautiful beaches on which giant tortoises can be seen (and saved) burying their eggs. All this is also true, but not the whole truth.

More than any other Central American country, Costa Rica resembles the first world. San José sports U.S.-like malls and shopping centers. People are accustomed to fastening their seatbelts, and it is fairly easy to find a nonsmoking restaurant. Public education is good, health care is free, and pensions are guaranteed There is a respect for privacy and for law and order that is encouraging—and also sometimes misleading. Ticos (the way Costa Ricans proudly refer to themselves and also the slightly derogatory or joking term used by their neighbors) are friendly to North Americans.

Along with all that is good, and even special, about the country, there are a number of somewhat hidden problems. Racism and elitism are rampant. The terrible poverty of other Latin countries is not found in Costa Rica, yet one-tenth of the country's population lives in absolute poverty. Malnutrition and obesity are on the rise. Alcoholism is a problem (an estimated 20 percent of Costa Rican adults have drinking problems). Crime is also on the upswing. And the natural paradise described in the tourist brochures hides a phenomenon of deforestation that means this land of once-virgin forests may soon have to import wood.

Although Costa Rica has no army and has prided itself in playing the role of mediator in the region, the rise of right-wing paramilitary groups in the 1980s clearly had tacit government support. The country's close relations with Taiwan, Israel, El Salvador during the worst of that country's genocidal war, and the United States belie the myth of perfect neutrality and peace.

A succession of Costa Rican administrations have taken class inequities seriously and have put forth important reforms that set it apart from its neighbors. At the same time, income and land distribution inequities have increased. Conflicted by this, in 1981 Costa Rica was the first underdeveloped country to suspend payment of its foreign debt. These days the overwhelming burden of debt so many poor countries bear has fueled international debate. Many governments have complained about the size of interest payments alone, and times of extreme national disaster in particular have pushed them to readdress the problem. But twenty years ago, Costa Rica's refusal was a brave and rather lonely one.

The crisis that pushed Costa Rica to this 1981 position has largely passed, but its consequences are reshaping the nation. A government that had committed itself to broad social welfare within capitalist parameters found itself unable to continue to fund its programs. Costa Rica's neighboring countries—El Salvador, Guatemala, Nicaragua— were mired in brutal wars. The United States needed Costa Rica to remain stable, to be its showcase for democracy. So from 1982 to 1990, the U.S. Agency for International Development (USAID) delayed the demand for debt repayment and pumped more than $1.3 billion in economic aid into Costa Rica. The World Bank and International Monetary Fund, also controlled by the United States, followed suit. What was less publicized was the fact that the United States agreed to delay its imposition of structural adjustment programs, which gave Costa Rica a time margin of freedom.

But just as monetary loans have their due dates, the time loan would eventually come due. Now it has. And this has brought problems. The country had opened its doors to all things American: investors, land speculators, tourists, even fugitives. Anything labeled Made in USA was valued in Costa Rica, which has two American Legion posts and an American Realty Company (which specializes in selling Costa Rican real estate to foreigners). Not just ordinary retirees but others whose histories may be more problematic have made their homes there. There are limits, however. U.S. citizen John Hull was finally indicted by a Costa Rican court in 1989 after the Iran-Contra hearings revealed what many already knew about the rancher's drug trafficking and arms running to the Contras.

Structural adjustment has now descended full force upon Costa Rica. Exports are on the rise, and the country's per capita income grew 10 percent between 1990 and 1994. The trade deficit widened, however, as the cost of imports increased and the value of exports declined. It's the same old story, suffered by every FMI- and World Bank–controlled country around the world. Costa Rica's foreign debt is now 20 percent higher than it was when it refused to pay it back in 1981.

In its class character and political agenda, the women's movement in Costa Rica resembles feminist movements in developed countries more than it does those of its neighbors—with the exception of Nicaragua. Issues such as sexual identity and homophobia, battering and violence against women in all its forms, job discrimination and sexual harassment are publicly debated. What's more, there are a number of organizations and projects that address these issues. And there is FIRE, the international women's radio program that María has run for more than a decade. Once only on shortwave radio, FIRE is now broadcasting as well via the Internet. Its reporters travel around the world, transmitting from wherever women struggle and tell their stories. FIRE is a creative, moving, powerful, and empowering chorus of women's voices.

The Costa Rican government has been pushed to pass legislation against the sexist use of women's bodies in commercial advertising, although the laws have been hard to enforce. San José had its first battered women's shelter in 1984, something unheard of in the region back then. Throughout the 1990s, the legal defense of women's rights was a priority; new laws have been passed, and the public defender's office devotes time and energy to cases brought. Yet battery, rape, and child abuse are on the rise. Abortion continues to be illegal, and sterilization remains the most common form of birth control. Teenage pregnancy is also on the rise. It is estimated that 25 percent of all Costa Rican women have their first child between the ages of fifteen and eighteen. One-fifth of these teenagers work as maids.

HONDURAS

Finally we come to Honduras, the home of one of our protagonists and the country in which both of them were kidnapped, disappeared, and tortured. Honduras, of all the countries on the isthmus, remains shrouded in mystery for most North Americans. Even during the 1980s, when news of El Salvador, Guatemala, and Nicaragua—however distorted—filled our daily papers and nightly news, Honduras remained cloaked in silence.

It was a deadly silence.

In 1997, when I traveled to Tegucigalpa to continue interviewing Nora, I could feel the ghosts of past abuse. Even arriving at the airport was an uneasy experience. I noticed how short the runway was and how close my plane had come to hitting a city overpass. Nora later told me that descending planes have collided with local street traffic on several occasions and that one of these accidents had involved a school bus full of children. The terminal itself was depressingly shabby, more so than those in the other Central American countries I had visited.

Yet I knew the United States had invested large sums of money in Honduras. Clearly this money had been poured into U.S. military bases and their Honduran counterparts; little if any had made its way to the civilian population.

To help create the conditions necessary to make Honduras into the base from which the United States would be able to subvert and put down the liberation struggles in Nicaragua, El Salvador, and Guatemala, the U.S. media in the early 1980s suddenly began talking about this Central American country as an oasis of peace and a model of democratization. No matter that these descriptions bore no resemblance to reality.

Honduras was vital to U.S. policy in Central America. It was centrally located and shared borders with the three countries then experiencing violent political conflict—conflict the Reagan and first Bush administrations wanted desperately to contain. And these administrations did contain those conflicts, using covert as well as overt methods, economic and diplomatic subversion as well as outright military attack. Honduras's Bay of Fonseca proved useful for these attacks, just as it had when the first Somoza had used it as a beachhead from which to attack Sandino's forces. Several land bases also became important in launching offensives against the rebels governing or fighting to govern other countries of the region.

Honduras itself, impoverished and burdened with an unpayable foreign debt, went along with the plan. The Honduran government, trampling its people in the process, literally began selling the country to foreign investors. More than any other Central American country, Honduras welcomed a large-scale invasion of manufacturers from Taiwan, Singapore, Hong Kong, and South Korea, with the resultant subhuman conditions for workers—especially for women—and the vast profits for overseas owners. In 1991, those laboring in the maquilas earned 48 U.S. cents an hour, making the country's labor costs the lowest in the region. The Honduran government even offered to sell Honduran passports to foreign investors at $25,000 each.

Honduras is about the size of Ohio, making it one of the larger countries on the isthmus. Its six million inhabitants are most densely congregated in its two major cities—Tegucigalpa, which is the capital, and San Pedro Sula, which is the more modern industrial center. The country has the advantage of two coastlines, with ports on the Atlantic (Caribbean) as well as the Pacific. Its rich indigenous history includes important Mayan archeological sites, but the vast majority of today's population considers itself mestizo.

Contradictions define the countries of Central America not only internally but also in the ways they are perceived externally. Especially by the U.S. press. So much depends on what information is disseminated and how. Compared with the tens of thousands of disappeared who have been documented throughout Guatemala's decades of civil war, the 80,000 civilian lives lost during El Salvador's long conflagration, and the ravages of Nicaragua's Contra war (which were coming to public attention because of the interest the Sandinista decade had generated internationally), human rights abuses in Honduras seemed almost insignificant. There, only 184 people were officially documented as disappeared. But this figure alone does not adequately project its history of horror.

During the last two decades of the twentieth century, local repressive (often paramilitary) forces as well as those of the other Central American countries operated with impunity in Honduras. Refugee camps and their environs were often sites of horrendous human rights abuses. Few of these made the international news, and when journalists tried to report them, their stories were ignored.

One such story, told to me recently by Nora Miselem herself, attests to what was going on and how it was being hidden. In the context of going over her testimony in this book, Nora recently wrote:

Speaking of life and death, there's an experience I want to talk about that I haven't mentioned before. It marked me terribly, perhaps because it involved the death of so many mothers, so many women. Witnessing this event made me feel like a criminal, because I couldn't legitimately give hope to the victims . . . even to one of the most vulnerable, a small child.

During the time I worked along the border, I saw all sorts of atrocities: U.S. soldiers training Honduran soldiers, for example, instructing them in counterinsurgency methods. I saw U.S. troops acting freely along our border with El Salvador, which was terrifying for refugees and for those of us trying to give those refugees humanitarian aid. We all saw how soldiers from various countries acted without restrictions on Honduran territory, how these soldiers came and went as if they were right at home.

One morning I saw a woman many months pregnant dead near one of the refugee camps. She'd been assassinated in the cruelest possible way, her throat slit and her body simply tossed like that on the ground. The word was that soldiers from the Honduran army had dragged her from the camp the night before, murdered her, and left her body there. There were also bullets in that woman's body, of the type used by our army. And that incident was one of many—women especially, raped and murdered, their bodies left for all to see. It was terribly painful for those of us who were trying to protect the refugee population and couldn't.

My own work in defense of the refugees' human rights, the public denunciations we made, accusing the offenders by name, generated official rage and no small amount of political persecution.

But I want to tell you about this one incident in particular. It happened in March of 1981. We were familiar with the official news campaigns in El Salvador, that tried to make the civil war appear like an imported struggle between the radical left—supported by the Soviet Union, so they said—and the extreme right. They tried to get us to believe that the Salvadoran government was caught in the middle, that it took a neutral position between right and left. Of course we knew better, but this campaign succeeded in confusing some sectors of society, especially children.

In March of that year some three thousand Salvadorans took refuge in Honduras. They fled, escaping repression in remote areas, bringing whole villages with them. When we noticed Honduran troop movement in the context of this immigration, we thought another massacre might be about to take place, like the one that had been carried out by the joint forces of Honduras and El Salvador at Río Sampul in May of 1980.

And we were right. This massacre was in the village of Los Hernández, La Virtud, in the department of Lempira near the Salvadoran border. After we received the great mass of refugees, we left them in an open field, exhausted and without shelter. Those of us whose job it was to protect the zone traveled to the Lempa River—to the place where the refugees had crossed over—in order to see if we could help those who had lagged behind: mostly the sick and wounded. The Honduran army had these people surrounded.

That night, when we returned with a little girl who had been badly wounded, as well as several women and one old man whom we'd managed to bring along, we came upon a painful piece of news. While we were out there trying to help those too weak to make it on their own, the Honduran army had entered that field and abducted fifteen young people. They murdered them with bullets and blows. And the rest of the refugees had been forced to witness this.

It was dark by the time we returned to the field. Overcome with the pain of what had taken place, I lay down at the entrance to the field, right there on the ground. I wanted to try to prevent the army from coming back in. A little Salvadoran boy, maybe eight years old, lay down beside me. And he asked: "Are you people at war too?" I couldn't answer. He was silent for a moment, as if confused, then he asked again: "Why are they killing us?" I found myself explaining the solidarity among our two peoples, but also the complicity of our armies.

Quickly he asked: "It's not true that the Russians are helping, is it?" It scared me to realize how that propaganda campaign had affected people, even innocent children. And I pulled myself together and told him no, that the Russians weren't helping. This child didn't say anything for a few moments and then, with great conviction, he asked me: "Don't you think we'd be better off dead?"

For me that little boy was The Little Prince. He couldn't understand the world of adults. I was an adult and I couldn't understand it either. Perhaps the worst part of all is that this massacre and all that went with it was thoroughly documented by a U.S. journalist whom I'd taken to the zone. He and his cameraman both witnessed everything that happened. He took his testimony to the U.S. Congress. But sometime later I saw this man again, and he told me they hadn't believed him! He had presented complete documentation: video footage of the people who were wounded, Salvadoran reconnaissance planes flying over Honduran territory, the bodies in the Lempa River . . . everything. They just didn't believe him.

With tremendous pain I had to accept the fact that the United States' foreign policy had generated so much violence that people had lost their capacity to distinguish between reality and fiction.

This story is typical of the atrocities that were perpetrated throughout Central America during the years of the dirty wars—atrocities often ignored, glossed over, or denied. It also attests to how few North Americans were privy to real news. Soon after the Sandinistas' 1979 victory in Nicaragua, U.S. military and economic aid began to flood Honduras. Long linked to the United States through the U.S.-owned banana enclaves, Honduras cemented a new relationship with Washington in the 1980s. In exchange for the use of its territory for U.S. counterinsurgency initiatives in the region, Honduras was a favored recipient of U.S. military and economic aid. During this period, Honduras was one of the world's top ten recipients of aid from the United States.

But this aid did not filter down to those in need. Levels of poverty, living conditions, education, employment, and prevalence of curable diseases remained the same as before. The U.S. ambassador to Honduras in those years, John Dimitri Negroponte, became a banana republic cold warrior. Like the others who are still with us—Henry Kissinger, Lawrence Eagleberger, et al.—Negroponte has a renewed presence in the current era of U.S. hegemony; his recent appointment to the United Nations does not bode well for our relationship to Central America—or the world.

DISAPPEARANCE

It is important that we stop for a moment and consider the phenomenon of disappearance that Nora's and María's stories sets before us.

The Holocaust was perpetrated primarily against Jews, but it was also perpetrated against Communists, Socialists, Romas (Gypsies), homosexuals, and others in central Europe at the midpoint of the twentieth century. It was an event that defied healthy imagination. We call it the Holocaust in deference to its enormity, and perhaps as a way of implying through such naming that nothing like it has happened before or since. Unspeakable as a particular social calamity may be, however, when it comes to human suffering, comparisons only tend to muddle the picture.

Today an insistent group of fascists, and in this country, some members of the extreme right wing, continue to claim that the Holocaust never happened. The vast majority of us who know that it did happen, and that it has and will happen again, vow to prevent its repetition at any cost. The most powerful deterrent continues to be the testimonies of survivors: their voices, visual images, memorabilia, and the monuments and museums erected so that succeeding generations will not forget. Whose heart can remain still before a mountain of human hair or the gold fillings taken from millions of teeth?

Memory is a powerful tool.

So we will not forget: it would be an unthinkable failure of the human spirit. Yet surely the assault by generations of Europeans against Native Americans was a holocaust of immense proportions, although it is still not officially recognized as such. The Africans brought to the Americas as slaves was surely another, although again, it is not officially recognized as such. The Armenian holocaust of 1915 preceded the Nazi assault by a quarter of a century. Most of us have never heard of it.

With each of these genocides there were those who vowed: we must not forget, this must not be repeated. But Indonesia followed, and Cambodia, then Guatemala, Palestine, Bosnia, the Kurds, Afghanistan, Rwanda: a succession of holocausts in which humans continued to massively abuse and murder other humans. Such horrors creep upon our consciousness one by one, too often garnering our response when it is already too late.

Reporting by contemporary media tends to dehumanize these events or to oversaturate us with their images. When we look at screen after screen of trenches of bodies, skeletal survivors, or the most recent in a long history of children's staring eyes and outstretched hands, they no longer seem real. Racism—our socially conditioned disdain for those different from ourselves—also keeps us from assimilating the single face, hearing the single voice. Individual stories bring these faces and voices to life.

If the victims are unable to articulate their experience (as the result of cultural fear, misplaced shame, the desire to forget, or the inaccessibility of viable outlets), evil also enjoys an unobstructed path. Eventually, if the news is not distorted, there may be a swell of international concern. Rescue missions may be undertaken (usually too late and far too meager). War tribunals may be established (usually underfunded, understaffed, and lacking far-reaching powers). Punishment and retribution often depend on the political interests of governments many thousands of miles distant. Information sputters, fades, and another horrifying event, somewhere else, claims our by now diminished attention.

Horror allowed to go unchecked numbs the human spirit.

To do its work, memory must be given voice. Victims must be allotted time and space (and often professional help) to work through the terror and reclaim as much of their physical and emotional integrity as possible. Stories must be told. And they must be the right stories. We, the witnesses, must listen, despite our increased conditioning that what takes place in distant lands and to people different from ourselves is no concern of ours.

Ours must also be an active listening, one that enables us to respond, to act.

Because the disappeared cannot speak, their stories have rarely been heard. And almost never in their own voices.

In a number of Latin American countries, from the late 1970s through the mid-1980s, this new type of holocaust called disappearance evolved and was highly refined; in isolated instances the practice continues to the present. Its perpetrators used many of their predecessors' methods: the rounding up of innocent citizens, massive or selective imprisonment, torture, rape, and murder. But they also employed a new modality, one that unleashed a new strategy of terror against entire populations.

Disappearance became a new word in the lexicon of horror.

No longer were we faced with ghettoization and transport to camps, where mass murder was made efficient and generations were able to claim they didn't know what was going on. Perhaps shrinkage of the globe during the latter half of the twentieth century has demanded that the perpetrators develop different strategies. Today it is much more difficult to keep large-scale death sites hidden.

Now, with disappearance, a man was snatched from his home here, a woman picked up off the street there, another abducted somewhere else. Always sudden, always unexpected. Small groups of nonpersons were moved from place to place. Tortured until these victims were of no further use alive, they were then summarily executed and relegated to remote and unmarked graves, or dropped from helicopters into volcanic craters or the sea.

He was disappeared; she was disappeared. The word became a reflexive verb: an event perpetrated upon its primary victim against his or her will, and also an event that profoundly, insistently, affected the larger community.[1] A person or persons were taken away under cover of night or in broad daylight on their way to work, and then literally erased—rendered invisible. Official records were often destroyed. The relentless perpetration against the victims, the mysterious act being committed, imbued the phenomenon with an additional quota of helplessness.

Often the disappeared were kept for months in clandestine prisons; sometimes they were taken from one to another; rarely were their whereabouts divulged. The most refined forms of torture became routine. And although most of the victims were never seen again, there were notable exceptions to this rule. In Uruguay, in elegantly appointed private clinics, some victims' mouths were sewn shut, layer by layer. Others had the incisors of wild animals implanted in their gums. The disfigured were then released into the general population, mute examples of what could and would be done to those who continued to rebel.[2]

Doctors attended interrogation sessions—complicit professionals who knew the human breaking point, how long someone might be expected to endure, when to stop a particular type of torture so the victim might regain some strength, only to be returned to the torture chamber in a few hours or days. These doctors, who had taken the same oath as health professionals everywhere to heal and do no harm, were also implicated in the repressive apparatus. Their crimes are reminiscent of those perpetrated by certain doctors in the Nazi death camp apparatus.

Family and friends who sought their loved ones were forced into their own syndrome of horror. As they went from prisons to hospitals to morgues and back, they repeatedly came up against a brutal wall of silence. No, he's not here. No, we have no record of her. I'm sorry, you must be mistaken. How can you be sure he didn't just run off with another woman? Rarely did a body appear (although sometimes they did appear, brutalized and mutilated—again as a warning to the public).

Occasionally, another prisoner might offer a brief message of hope; he or she had seen a face, heard a name, or recognized a muted scream, offering fresh conjecture that the disappeared person might still be alive. And hope and its feverish counterpart of activity would be renewed—only to be stretched thin and dashed once more.

Sheila R. Tully, in her examination of disappearance in Nicaragua, succinctly describes the phenomenon. She might as easily be speaking of its effects in Guatemala, El Salvador, or Honduras:

> The impact within a family is devastating. Each story told by a wife, sister or mother begins with the routine of the everyday. Quickly, that is smashed. The rupture—the disappearance—occurs and nothing is ever the same. . . . The primary goal of the mothers is to learn exactly what happened to their disappeared relatives. Are they alive or dead? If they are dead, where and how did they die? It is the details that are important. . . . "Can you tell me what happened when your son disappeared?" I asked one woman in her fifties. "Which one?" The matter-of-factness of her response unnerved me.[3]

Over the years, some bodies have been found. Most have not. Mothers of one, two, three, or more disappeared still seek their children's whereabouts.

During the two decades of the dirty wars in Latin America, tens of thousands of men and women were disappeared in Argentina (30,000), Chile (20,000), Uruguay, Paraguay, Haiti, Colombia, Venezuela, Bolivia, Brazil, Mexico, and Peru.

Central America offers similar statistics. In El Salvador, since the 1980s, 7,000 cases of disappeared persons have been reported. Guatemala is the Central American country with the highest number of disappeared: more than 40,000 since the 1960s. In Honduras, 185 men and women have been disappeared since the early 1980s.[4] Nicaragua has a more complicated history because the decade of Sandinista rule (1979–1990) separates a repressive past from the current period in which disappearances are being documented once again. The Nicaraguan Human Rights Center has files on some 900 disappeared, whereas other sources claim as many as 7,000 (of whom nothing is known about 5,000).

Panama might have escaped this sad history had it not been for the U.S. invasion of that country on December 20, 1989. After the attack, a single cemetery was said to contain the bodies of 120 victims, and this became the official figure of those who lost their lives. But reputable sources testify to at least twelve mass graves in which many more are believed to lie. There are stories of bodies incinerated and tossed into the sea; many were disposed of before proper identification could be made. These are Panama's disappeared. Hospital records listing names of the wounded treated during and just after the invasion have also mysteriously disappeared, and the corporate media—in Panama as well as in the United States—have largely ignored the situation. Unlike other Central American nations, in Panama there is no evidence that disappearance was a systematic practice carried out over a period of time. But several thousand Panamanians may have died as a result of the U.S. invasion, and the number of disappeared is still unknown.

Only Costa Rica and Belize were able to avoid the terror.

All these numbers are approximate, most likely conservative estimates. Of the 185 officially documented cases of persons disappeared in Honduras, Nora and María put two faces to the statistic. They are among the 5, out of the 185, who survived.

As it emerged into public consciousness, disappearance was condemned by organizations of international stature. The Organization of American States (OAS), in article 4 of its Resolution No. 666 (November 18, 1983), declared that "in [Latin] America the practice of forcibly disappearing people is an affront to the conscience of the Hemisphere, and constitutes a crime against humanity." The United Nations Working Group on Forced and Involuntary Disappearance stated in its 1986 report that "The forced and involuntary disappearance practiced in our time constitutes the negation of the most basic of human rights; it causes infinite harm to its victims, profound social and psychological problems for their families, and demoralizes the societies in which it occurs. This is a truly horrendous human rights violation that merits the attention of the international community."

Since these declarations, governments have begun to hold one another accountable for human rights violations, and some—at least insofar as their discourse was concerned—have begun to look at such violations when considering diplomatic and trade relations. Human rights conventions were established. International organizations, such as the United Nations High Commission for Refugees (ACNUR),

Amnesty International, and America's Watch (later called Human Rights Watch Americas), were set up to evaluate human rights abuses throughout the world. And in specific countries, when dictatorships or other forms of authoritarian government produced periods of particularly brutal state-imposed violence, local organizations also kept watch. During the twentieth century, the subject of human rights was put on the agenda, and governments have felt obliged to pay lip service, at least, to internationally agreed-upon standards.

Throughout Central and Latin America, these organizations began recording and investigating cases of disappearance. Groups of family members—particularly women, particularly mothers—sprang up in several capitals, eventually coming together in a continent-wide movement. The members of all these institutions and groups have demanded to know what was done with their loved ones. If nothing else, they want bodies, accountability, retribution—when the idea of retribution itself may be unthinkable.

The Mothers and Grandmothers of the Plaza de Mayo in Buenos Aires are the best known, although they are not the only such group.[5] They are sometimes referred to as *las locas*, the crazy women. Grief and rage have made them mad, and madness has kept them alive.

Disappearance and memory. Over the past two decades and throughout Latin America, mothers holding photographs of their missing children have become a familiar sight. This reproduction of a beloved face—sometimes a hand-tinted studio portrait in an elaborate frame, more often a tiny ID shot, faded and torn—may be the only physical image through which those left behind can manifest their grief.

Disappearance as strategy and tactic responds to a number of objectives on the part of the terrorist regime. When bodies bear the marks of torture, or a single bullet hole in the forehead gives lie to the claim that a prisoner was shot while trying to escape, disposing of the body in an unmarked grave eliminates the need for embarrassing explanations. With disappearance, no official record exists. Those responsible cannot be traced.

Family members and friends who are kept busy searching for their loved ones obviously also have less time in which to organize other sorts of resistance. Their ongoing search has, in fact, become a new and all-consuming category of resistance. But most important, disappearance is an effective form of repression against an entire population; the widespread uncertainty, insecurity, and fear it generates keep people permanently off balance and in a state of despair. There is a recognizable pathology: a kind of collective unnerving ensues. Recent history has allowed us to name this unnerving—post-traumatic stress disorder. Psychology most often applies the diagnosis to individuals, but I contend it is applicable to populations as well.

Still, repressive governments and their quasi-legal paramilitary groups consistently underestimate the strength and determination of popular memory, and the lengths to which people will go in their quest for justice. Over time, as it became more difficult to hide the conditions of life and deepening inequalities in these countries, regimes became embarrassments even to their long-term overseas supporters. Superficial or sometimes more meaningful changes were made. More democratic forms of government were ushered into power. People began to speak out. Mass graves were discovered, bodies exhumed, identities established, some form of justice promised. International solidarity joined domestic efforts to bring the murderers to public scrutiny.

With the weakening of the Pinochet regime in Chile, a vast field of identical black metal crosses was discovered in Santiago's General Cemetery. All these crosses bore the letters N.N. (*ningún nombre*, or no name) and were revealed to be the markers of hundreds of burials. Mass graves hidden in other parts of the country have also gradually been identified and opened. Such clandestine graves have been unearthed in a number of Latin American countries.

In a few of these—Argentina, Uruguay, and Chile—different models for bringing the perpetrators to justice have been attempted. The efforts usually have reached only into the middle ranks of the military. Few of the men at the top have so far been tried, and few convicted. There have been no internationally recognized Nuremberg trials for the Stroesners or Pinochets or Videlas, the Somozas or Trujillos.[6] In

some cases, one or another form of economic redress has been legis-
lated. Occasionally a torturer himself, sometimes from the safety of
another country, comes forward with testimony about his crimes, the
weight of his conscience finally having become unbearable.[7]

During the era of unchecked dictatorship in Latin America, these
brutal regimes had free reign. Because their enforced stability provided
much sought-after foreign markets and favored our balance of trade,
the United States accepted and in many cases actively supported such
governments. Republican and, yes, also Democratic administrations
have too often characterized themselves by a human rights discourse
masking policies that put greed above humanitarian concern. In recent years, this dichotomy between discourse and policy has become
ever more sophisticated.

Only when local Central American struggles had reached levels that
could no longer be ignored, and solidarity activists succeeded in transmitting the news, did truth surface—although usually to audiences
or readerships composed of the already informed. Eventually, international public opinion managed to crack conspiratorial layers of silence. When change seemed inevitable, our State Department reacted
to this pressure and, in line with our stated policy of support for democracy around the world, threatened minor reprisals. Or the United
States entered into negotiations that positioned it more favorably.

The establishment press has become more effectively complicit in
keeping international news coverage spotty, scandal-centered, and
lacking in continuity—as well as biased on the side of first world ex-
perts. We rarely hear from those directly involved, those who lived in
these countries and endured their realities. And so we in the United
States know little about Central America. The larger more powerful
nations farther south might capture our headlines for a day or week,
then fade from sight once more. But the smaller countries of the isthmus, so geographically close, only come to our attention in the context
of the waves of new refugees, or when a war that perhaps has been raging for decades explodes with an incident that briefly makes the news.

In the mining communities of Chile and Bolivia there have been periodic massacres of thousands. There have been full-scale revolutions

and put-downs of those revolutions—invariably directed and financed by U.S. covert forces—in both of these countries as well as in Guatemala (1954), Dominican Republic (1965), Nicaragua (1980–1989), Colombia, Peru, and Mexico (all ongoing). Throughout the region, local opponents of all of these regimes have been disappeared.

Nora Miselem and María Suárez were kidnapped and disappeared for less than two weeks in 1982. Most of the Latin Americans disappeared during the 1970s and 1980s were never seen again. Stories might come down of a brief glimpse of someone in a military hospital bed or a voice overheard on the other side of a cell wall.[8] Mass graves have been discovered and opened; bones sometimes have been identified and proper burials performed. In a few cases the testimony of others has provided some closure to years of anguished wait.

The continued absence of the vast majority of the disappeared has permanently scarred the face of the continent, however, leaving in each country questions that will forever remain unanswered, families that will never again be whole, bodies that cannot be mourned. The tension between knowing and not knowing continues to shape each nation's politics, social organization, culture, and interpersonal relationships. Those left behind have been changed. If they are angry, theirs is a different kind of anger. If resigned, their resignation wears a different face. We who did not live this history can sympathize, but we cannot know how it operates within a body, how it eats away at the human spirit.

That is, we were unable to come close to understanding until September 11, 2001, when Islamic fundamentalist terrorists hijacked four commercial airliners and used their own bodies as well as those of the passengers on those planes as human weapons. When they flew into New York's World Trade Center twin towers, the Pentagon in Washington, D.C., and were forced down in a field in rural Pennsylvania, the impacts together with the explosion of jet fuel disappeared thousands of human beings—literally vaporized them into nothingness. Suddenly people in the United States knew something about disappearance: the body forever gone, nothing tangible left to mourn.

There are, however, important differences between our experience and that of our Latin American counterparts. Both sorts of disappearance are politically motivated. Both are monstrous. But in the attacks of September 11, we knew our loved ones were dead. Even without bodies, after the first few days and weeks, the element of uncertainty no longer strangled the grieving process. In the tens of thousands of kidnappings in Latin America during the 1970s and 1980s, mourning was forever delayed. Third-person testimony, a word here or there, kept hope—however faint—alive. As families continued to search for their loved ones, attempted to find out what had happened to them, the collective agony was prolonged, often for years.

Another difference is that the terrorists who attacked the United States on September 11 were from other countries, other cultures. The terrorists who kidnapped, tortured, and disappeared so many throughout Latin America were almost always from the same countries as their victims; brother against brother and (to a lesser extent) sister against sister. This was a particular form of genocide. With the attacks that disappeared so many in the United States, government agencies attended to victims' families; in Latin America, governments were complicit with, if not the perpetrators of, these crimes.[9]

A third difference is the fact that in the wake of the September 11 attacks, an entire nation came together to mourn. The victims' grief and rage found solace in the grief and rage of the national community. Those in power organized vigils and led the fight against terrorism. The families and friends of the disappeared in Latin America were forced to grieve and rage in silence. Their governments had taken their loved ones and intended to victimize them as well.

I know a Chilean woman, not much older than myself, who lost five of her six children. The sixth became emotionally ill. Throughout much of Latin America, post-traumatic stress disorder has become a national disease.

In Montevideo, Uruguay, members of a third generation that calls itself Los Hijos (the Sons and Daughters) recently covered the face of an upscale apartment building with graffiti announcing the presence of a particular known torturer now living on one of its floors. Other stories have begun to appear that defy traditional expectations of family and community interaction. For example, the DNA work still being carried out by the Grandmothers of the Plaza de Mayo has unearthed a third generation of disappeared: the sons and daughters who were born to those kidnapped and murdered three decades ago. At the time small children and infants, some of whom had been born in clandestine prison cells to mothers dying of torture, they were stolen and/or adopted by military families unable to bear children of their own. Thus the children of revolutionaries unknowingly have grown up in the homes of those who murdered their parents.

In their tireless attempts to locate these children—their grandchildren—the Grandmothers have developed a sophisticated DNA databank. Some fifty or sixty disappeared children have been identified to date, and many have been willing to meet with members of their original families. Some always suspected they didn't belong where they were and themselves sought out the Grandmothers. Others, even when found, have not wanted to allow this new set of questions and answers into lives they prefer to keep uncluttered by unwelcome emotions. The Grandmothers have had to devise compassionate ways of dealing with situations for which there are few if any models.

This brief overview of the phenomenon of disappearance likely mutes considerably more than it reveals. In the U.S. media, news flashes generally emphasize first world interpretations of third world realities. People's lives are largely absent from such reports. In countries such as those mentioned here, large Indian populations and other disenfranchised groups have been all but silenced. And within the diversity of human populations, the voices of women are heard least of all.

Now I had borne witness to two women as they revealed histories that joined into one. In María's story, in Nora's story, and in the many ways they weave together, we hear voices that are unusual in several important ways. Each, out of her own experience of struggle in male-dominated political organizations, nurtured within herself a woman's strength she could draw on in a situation in which it would make the difference between death and survival. Yet each, after her ordeal—

because of fear or ongoing political work—was forced into many years of silence. Silence with others, which naturally includes silence with oneself. Even several years after the events of 1982, when Nora and María found themselves at the same meeting in Managua, they dared not speak of what they had shared for fear it could affect their current political activity.

Several more years were necessary. The balance of power in the world had to change dramatically. Latin American feminists had to begin to question their own place in struggle, and the secrets they had been forced to keep, before giving voice to this sort of experience was a choice they were able to make.

Once speaking out became an option, certain conditions also had to be created. The mixed political organizations of the 1970s and 1980s, however much some of them had grown and changed, still offered little space for such stories. We women, crossing class, racial, sexual, party, and national lines, had to create this space. We alone understood its importance. We claimed it as necessary—not only to ourselves but to future generations.

Even after the telling, Nora's and María's stories don't have neatly wrapped endings. They do not provide perfect answers. Rather, they point a way, delineate a journey. Some damage doesn't heal. Both these women are different today than they were before the summer of 1982. Stronger, perhaps, but also more vulnerable. And more willing to assume that vulnerability. Powerful feminists, they continue to ponder the issues of voice and silence, mandate and transgression, oppression and the complex roads that lead away from its grasp.

Despite her ongoing human rights work, trauma still seeps from every one of Nora's pores. Her beloved husband died of lung cancer about a year after our work on this book. Her life was further affected by the ravages of Hurricane Mitch, which left her widowed mother homeless. Nora lives in Tegucigalpa with her teenage daughter and son, ever hopeful that a new Honduran administration may decide to bring her kidnappers to justice. She wants this as a way of honoring those who did not survive; their unheard voices are more important to her than her own.

María coordinates FIRE, the Feminist International Radio Endeavor, an important alternative global exchange of women's voices out of Costa Rica. For more than a decade, FIRE has been broadcasting daily and from almost every corner of the world.[10] María also continues to teach and give workshops in a variety of venues, even as in 2002 she completed an advanced degree in journalism. She shares her life with a woman whose communication interests mirror her own; they live and work for periods in the United States and for periods in María's little house in the Costa Rican countryside.

What both Nora and María went through informs the ways in which they see the world, struggle to love and work, bear witness so that the silences continue to shatter and the truth emerge. Because each has seen the other mirrored in her own face, and has given voice to that mirroring, they also help us to look into the mirrors looking back at us, and to make the choices that honor both living and dead.

Now it was time for me to visit Nora and María in their countries, to ask them to probe their memories for other parts of their stories. In April 1997 I traveled to Tegucigalpa and San José.

FIVE

NORA

Tegucigalpa's airport, even in the spring of 1997, was an old, inadequate structure at the end of a runway that threatened to collide with city streets. I'd heard the story about the plane that overshot its mark and hit a school bus. Nora wasn't there to meet me, and I waited in and then outside the terminal building, thinking about the sinister events I knew had taken place here not that many years before. Then I saw her old car and her expansive smile behind the wheel. We drove to her modest but modern home in a residential area on the outskirts of the city. The next few days would be morning-to-night conversation, recorded as Nora lit one cigarette with the one extinguishing itself between her expressive fingers.

One day I asked to be taken to the scene of Nora's abduction. She preferred we take a cab and had the driver let us off several blocks away. As we made our way to the spot—that pedestrian-only block in downtown Tegucigalpa—I could feel her mounting tension. Nora reenacted the events of fifteen years before, pointing out the shop window she'd wondered if she was strong enough to break, where the vehicle had stopped, the order of things as she remembered them.

That same day we visited the building where María and the other comrades had been captured. Once it had been a small apartment block, but it now houses offices. Even when Nora said she had once lived there, the guard at the gate wouldn't let us in.

Most of our time we spent taping, sometimes in the sunny downstairs living room of Nora's home, occasionally—when I sensed she

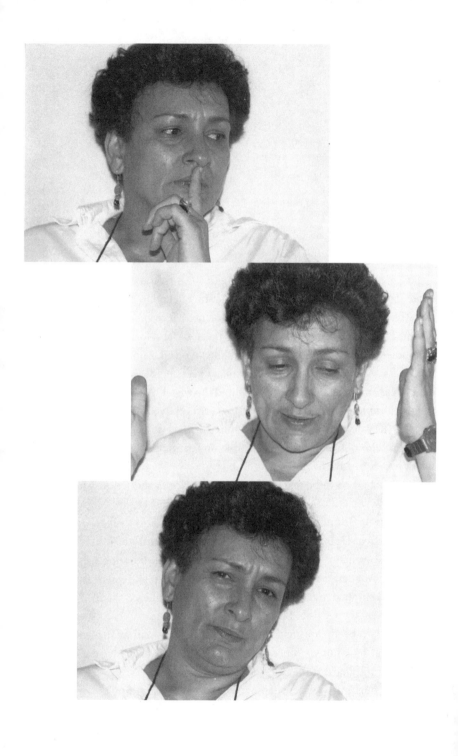

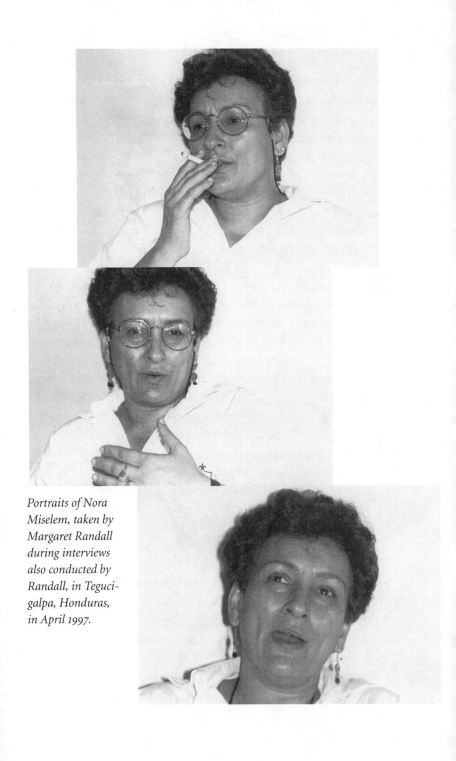

Portraits of Nora Miselem, taken by Margaret Randall during interviews also conducted by Randall, in Teguci-galpa, Honduras, in April 1997.

wanted to try to explore her memory more deeply—in a tiny study on the roof. No one would interrupt us there. We were alone, then, the two of us with the images that haunt this woman every day and night, the pack of cigarettes never far from her fingertips, and my tape recorder.

During our interview in Managua, Nora had talked about her first child, a little boy who died in unexplained and troubling circumstances during the first years of her political involvement. She'd referred to his death as if it had been an accident, but I wasn't so sure. So when we sat down together to begin this next stage of interviewing, I asked her to begin there.

Well, I can sum it up, give you an idea of what happened. When I left the university, I knew I was being watched. I knew that there was surveillance on many of us here in Honduras—women as well as men. For that reason, I decided to leave home. My parents spent much of their time in San Pedro Sula, but they also had a place here. And I decided to move from the house they kept here to another neighborhood where I wouldn't be known.

When I moved I naturally took my son with me. Two months later, I was playing with him one day—he had just turned two—and I happened to think: my mother took him to a doctor on a regular basis, just for checkups, that sort of thing. And I thought I should take him too. Some time had gone by since he'd had a physical. So I went looking for a doctor, a doctor who was a family friend. And, you know, I wasn't even giving my son vitamins. He was such a healthy child, very intelligent, with such vitality, such energy, very loving . . .

Anyway, I went looking for this doctor—my son was playing happily, I remember—and they told me he wasn't in. That he was at a particular hospital, here in the city. So I went over there, and although the doctor I was looking for wasn't there, there were others of course. I was told there were other doctors who were perfectly acceptable. So I asked one of them to look at my boy.

At first we were in, well I guess you'd call it an examining room. I remember my son was beside me, and every once in a while he'd tug at me and say: Mami, let's go, let's get out of here. When he'd see them giving shots to other children, things like that. The whole thing happened so fast.

The thing is, at a particular moment someone came and gave my son a shot too. I asked: Why are you injecting him? I've just brought him in for a check-up, there's nothing wrong. . . . It was a nurse, a black nurse I remember, and she said she had orders, orders from a doctor. But no doctor had seen my son at that point. Everything happened very fast.

I remember calling the family of my son's father. They had a family friend, a doctor too, who had seen my boy and confirmed there was nothing wrong with him. Nothing at all. He'd never had health problems of any kind. But for some reason they were going to do an x-ray. And I had my son in my arms. He'd received the injection quite some time before. My son was curious about the x-ray machinery, he was asking questions about it, and I was telling him: Look, we're going in a few minutes. I told him we were going to visit a little friend of his, another boy he liked a lot. We're going home, I told him, and then we'll go see so and so. . . .

In the midst of all this, another nurse came and grabbed him from me. She just took him. I can't even remember what she was saying at that point. I think I went into shock about then, and I can't remember what she told me. All I know is that she took my son and ran out of the room. She shut the door behind her. And I kept asking: What's going on? What's going on? I think I was confused and scared because she closed the door.

Finally I walked out of that room and tried to follow them, where they'd taken him. What I saw was my son, tied down at the wrists, and someone—I think it was an intern—trying to revive him. That's when I realized that his heart had stopped, that he'd gone into cardiac arrest.

I simply approached where they all were, but I was in a state of shock. I can't really explain it. I couldn't understand what was going on. That's when they told me that my son was dead. And I just kept saying: But that can't be! How . . . how . . . They kept telling me he was dead, and that they'd have to perform an autopsy.

But, understand, moments before I'd held my child in my arms. We were talking, normally. I couldn't believe what I was hearing! How could I believe it? All I remember now is that I picked up my son's body, and I began to pace back and forth, to walk with him. And I began calling people. My ex-sister-in-law was one of the first to arrive. And I remember saying to her: Look, he's alive. He's moving. But she just looked at me and said: No, he isn't. He's dead.

It was as if it was impossible for me to accept what had happened. Then I remembered that right after they'd given him that shot, one of the doctors had come up to me and asked if he'd taken something at home, something he shouldn't have. Or what had happened to him. Did he fall, he asked. I didn't understand what he was talking about. But I called home, just to make sure he hadn't taken anything, that nothing had happened. I didn't know if maybe he'd found some pills of some kind, some medication that belonged to someone else, and swallowed it without my knowledge. But the people at the house where we'd been staying told me no, they didn't think anything like that had happened.

So, what can I say? I was in a state of total shock. From this perspective, now, I know that I should have authorized the autopsy. At least we would have known. But at the time, I couldn't do that. I just wasn't prepared. It was all so sudden.

From then on, I can't even remember the exact order of things. My son's funeral was one of the worst experiences of my life. The political situation made it impossible for us to hold the wake at my parents' home or at the place where we'd been staying. We had to have it at a funeral parlor.

What kept going through my head at the time was how my son had been alive one moment and dead the next. Just like that. I didn't even really understand that he was dead. I didn't want to accept it, not for a long time. For months and months I had terrible nightmares. And I didn't want to bury him, because I was sure he was still alive. Finally, I couldn't bear to put him in the earth, so I buried him above ground, in one of those cemetery walls, near where my older brother was.

I had these nightmares every night. I'd wake up crying, because in my dreams I imagined that I was digging him up, that I was digging at the earth with my bare hands, and I would find him alive. And then I'd run with him, we'd run together. . . . It was horrendous to wake from those dreams.

This all reflected the fact that I hadn't wanted to bury him. I couldn't bear it. And I was in a terrible state for a long time. Such pain. It was so hard for me to understand or accept what had happened. I'd invent my own defense mechanisms—what can I say? My son was fascinated with the moon. So when he died I also became fixated on the moon. I thought he had become the moon. I just wanted to see him materialized as something tangible.

A death like that is impossible to understand. I kept remembering how, when he'd seen another child at that hospital get a shot, he'd pulled at me and said: Mami, let's go. What can I say? I was in a terrible state, for a long, long time. I know that death is only a physical separation. Mothers from their children . . . any of us from the people we love. But I kept inventing mechanisms through which I might be able to feel my son's presence.

I was twenty-six at the time. Two months after my son's death I still hadn't touched any of his things. They were all just as he'd left them. His tricycle was right there on the patio of the house where we'd been staying. It was awful when I got back from the burial and saw the things that had belonged to him, a couple of little blankets he'd been playing with, stuff like that: his mosquito netting, the musical mobile that hung above his bed. He used to sleep with me. He had his own crib, but he liked sleeping with me.

What was I saying? Oh, yes, I'd be talking about whatever, with someone, and all of a sudden I'd find myself talking about him. One day one of my sisters-in-law, who is a psychologist, she told me: You know, Norita, it might be a good idea for you to see a psychologist, get a little help. So I took her advice. I went to see a psychologist at a private clinic, here in Tegucigalpa.

Actually, I went several times. And the psychologist eventually decided to hospitalize me for five or six days. He was hoping I might be able to get through the trauma. He said he thought I was stuck, unable to move through my fixation with my son's death, my nightmares and all. As it turned out, I had those nightmares for years.

But I did go into that clinic for a few days. The doctor would come to see me for brief moments, once or twice a day. He said I could do whatever I wanted, except that he wouldn't let me bring a photograph of my son with me, or anything that had belonged to him. Because I tended to lose myself looking at his toys, touching them, going through his clothing, smelling his scent that was still there on his things. . . .

So that's where I was, in that clinic, when suddenly one day the same nurse showed up, the black nurse who had been at the public hospital and had given my son that shot. I have no idea how she knew I was there. I was sitting there one day and she just appeared.

And, I remember, it was never like me to hurt someone else's feelings, to attack their sensibilities. At that point in my life I had a very gentle nature, not like now. But that nurse appeared, and I remember wondering how she knew where to find me. And she began talking to me, telling me that she too had children, two children. It was clear that she'd come expressly to talk to me about my child.

Then she started talking to me about God, about God's will, and suddenly I got angry. I told her to leave. Get out, I said, your God is not my God. That's what I said. And that sort of reaction wasn't usual for me in those days. But I must have sensed there was something strange about that nurse just showing up like that. And I rejected her totally. Especially when I got it that she was trying to console me, console me with talk about her God.

I spent those few days at that clinic, and then I came home. And I continued to live my life. But several months later, in another safe house, I found myself thinking back to that scene. And then of course much later, when I was in the clandestine prison and this guy was torturing me, and he also said: You know why your son died, don't you? Because you've got yourself involved in all this shit. And don't you forget, your parents are still alive. . . . I understood that he was threatening me.

I knew that Nora hadn't been married to her first child's father, and I asked her to tell me something about her relationship with this man and the pregnancy that ensued.

Well, we have to go back to my time at the university. And I'm going to tell you something. Because there are times when I look at my daughter, at the education we've been able to give her, and I feel very proud. Amazed and proud. I was twenty-three when I became pregnant with my first child, and I didn't have the courage or the determination in those days to walk into a pharmacy and ask for birth control pills. I was too embarrassed!

I was only actually with the father of my first child on four occasions, and fully dressed. What can I say? Before that, I'd had a relationship with a North American named Owen, I think I told you about him, a man I really admired and liked. That was in 1975. For several years following that first relationship I didn't date. I still felt a lot for that first man in my life.

So I wasn't really looking. I wasn't in the mood, and I didn't feel attracted to anyone else. But then I met this guy, and he impressed me. Well, I remember one thing that didn't impress me so much, and that was the way he had of trying to get my attention. He'd see me walk by and he'd call out: Pssst, pssst . . . I'd look up, and it would be him. That annoyed me, that way he had of calling out to me. He'd been in Argentina, he'd spent a few years there, and he had this aggressive way of trying to get my attention.

But still, in spite of the fact that we belonged to two different student organizations, and we were super sectarian in those days, we did notice one another. Oh, my, the Right had such an easy time of it with us! We did their work for them. They didn't even have to do us in; we on the Left were so sectarian back then that we did ourselves in. I'm talking about 1977: sectarianism everywhere.

It was terrible. We were all guilty of it. But anyway, this man and I began noticing one another at the different political activities that took place on campus, no? And he impressed me, he did, I must admit it. Plus, I don't know why, but I always associated him with my older brother, the one who had died of cancer. It was a strange association. They didn't even look alike. My brother had strong Arabic features. His eyebrows, his eyes, his face. But there was something, maybe in his manner, I don't know, because this guy was very Indian looking, his features were very indigenous. They really didn't look alike at all. But there was something there, a connection.

So we began to date, but clandestinely. No one could know. Because we belonged to these two opposing organizations. My comrades thought of him as crazy—ultra-leftist they called him. But we found ways of seeing one another. We'd meet off campus, and he'd give me a cassette with my favorite music on it, or an apple, whatever. I got pregnant the first month we were together.

It wasn't something I'd planned. It wasn't something I'd even thought about. It was a result of my ignorance, that's all. When my period didn't come, I was frightened. Mostly I was thinking about my father, what he would say. So I told my older sister first. I wanted to see how she would react. And she responded beautifully.

She just kept saying: Oh how wonderful! She never asked me if I was planning on getting married. She just told me that she would be there for me, to help in any way she could. Which made me feel a little better. And then I also told the guy, my child's father. We saw one another at an activity, I remember, and I got him alone and told him: I think I'm pregnant. And he too reacted well. He started making plans, telling me how happy he was.

But then I went to a doctor, who confirmed that I was indeed pregnant. And that's when it really hit me. I began to think about the great responsibility of having a child. I knew being a mother was going to change my life, and I started thinking about whether or not I would be able to continue at the university.

I remember some of my cousins were also at the university then, and I'd try to avoid them, especially when I began to show. Then I got fed up with having to try to do that. It's my life, I told myself. My mother had accepted it already. I'd gone to San Pedro to talk with her. She was fine. She began talking about how it would be: your sister Rosita is going to have a baby, too. She can pass her baby clothes along to you. That sort of thing. And my mother helped me tell my father.

But something happened around that time, something with the father of my child, that made me stop and think about what I was doing.

Was it worth it, I asked myself, to continue to go through this with him? I understood the responsibility of bringing a child into this world, and so I simply decided to do it on my own. I decided not to count on his support. I guess I figured it would be enough to take care of one child without having to take care of two.

I had this friend who was a pilot, and I asked him if he would fly me to San Pedro. He did, and I went to talk to my mother again. I remember, I was vomiting, and she was vomiting right along with me! She kept saying, but you can get married and then divorced. She wanted to keep things legitimate; you know how mothers are. But she couldn't convince me. I kept saying no, why would I do that?

Finally she understood, but there was still my father to contend with. One day I heard her telling him: Selim, you need to know. Nora got married, and her husband wants to take her away to live in Argentina. She knew how to handle the situation. My father started begging me, like a little boy: Mama, he said, stay here. Don't leave. And I pretended to consider his request. Okay, I finally said, I won't go.

I spent that vacation with my family. But then I thought, now more than ever I can't leave the university. I can't stop my studies. I have to finish, especially with this new responsibility. So I stayed in school. What else can I tell you? Everything changed the moment my son was born.

As Nora spoke of her parents' reaction to her first pregnancy, I wondered about their ability to accept it in such a positive way. I knew that they had both come from more or less conventional Arabic families and that, in the context of Honduras in the mid-twentieth century, social influences would have conspired against this easy acceptance. I also knew Nora's parents loved her unconditionally.

My mother's reaction to my having my first child was really interesting. You're right; both my parents come from a more or less conventional Arabic background. But my mother's mother was a woman from the Honduran countryside. My grandmother became a widow at the age of eighteen, a widow with two children. She had my mother and

another child, a son. They lived in a very poor area. My maternal grandfather had a great deal of property in the south of the country, but when
he died my grandmother was left with nothing.

My mother grew up wanting to be a nun. My father, on the other
hand, was the son of Arabs who had settled in Honduras. He also
wanted a religious life. He studied with English Jesuits for a time. But
they met, and it really was love at first sight. And I think this was important in my life, and the lives of my sister and brother: we were all
the products of a really extraordinary love. A love like that is capable
of carrying people through a lot.

*Love. A love capable of carrying people through a lot, including the hor-
rendous events she would later experience. I told Nora I couldn't imagine
it had been easy for her parents, knowing their daughter had been raped
by torturers, threatened with firing squads and more, to reconcile themselves to that. Had it been love alone that had helped them through the
difficult time after her disappearance? How had they, not political mili-
tants but loving parents, been able to cope, to deal with all that? How were
they able to go on living, walk the same streets, breathe the same air, in
the place where their daughter had suffered such abuse?*

It's had terrible consequences, especially for my father. I'll tell you, for
example, when I got home after being disappeared. . . . Well, first of
all I must tell you that my mother dreamt my kidnapping before it
happened.

I remember: I didn't go right home. María and I and the others, first
we went to the warehouse where my father's business was. And my
mother immediately took charge of the situation. It was she who accompanied María to the airport. It was she who helped one of the
other prisoners. She dealt with everything. She's a strong woman,
extraordinary. . . .

And I'll tell you something else. Here in Honduras abortion is something you simply cannot talk about. Abortion for any reason, even when
there's been a pregnancy caused by rape. But my mother has her own
ideas. She's a very special person. My grandmother, like I told you, at

the age of eighteen was forced to come from the countryside to the city. And she had to take in other people's laundry in order to support her two children. My mother had a hard life when she was a child.

Whenever my mother would tell me about what her mother went through, she'd say: it would have been better if she'd had an abortion. And as I say, that's just not something you say here. But my mother was always very clear. She'd ask, why bring children into this world to suffer? One should only have the children one is able to provide for. And that wasn't the usual attitude here. Much more often you'd hear someone say: it doesn't matter if you have ten children, God will provide.

My mother is different. She has her own ideas about life. I remember when I got out of that prison and came home to my family, my father was loving, he was supportive, but he would fall silent for long periods of time. He couldn't speak.

And later, just before he died, when I came back from exile in Nicaragua, he didn't really want to go out much by then, but I got him to let me take him to a place here in the southern part of the country, a place called Ojojona. It's not far from Tegucigalpa, a very picturesque little town.

I had to lie and tell him that a friend, someone he really loved, was waiting for us there. That's the only way I was able to get him to go. He'd be all nervous, fearful really, and I'd be watching him. By that time it was as if he'd already said goodbye to the world, like he didn't want to go anywhere, to make contact with anything new.

You know, the same thing happens to me at times. It's as if I get tired of looking at the world, tired of seeing. Maybe it's that I don't like what I see. And I feel like shutting myself away.

I still wanted to know if, after surviving the disappearance and going home to her parents, Nora had been able to describe in detail her experience of torture. Had she tried to spare them or had she shared it all?

I did talk to them. I did tell them the details. And that's the first time I noticed my father in that attitude of sort of disconnecting himself from the world. I know that my imprisonment marked my father's disconnection from the world. It was the first time I saw that in him. I was talking about the torture, yes.

When I got there, to where they were, my mother was pulling at her hair. Imagine, she'd been to one morgue after another, looking for me, looking. She had her back to me, and she was pulling at her hair. I said: Mama. (My father used to call my mother and me both Mama, we never knew which one of us he was calling.) I said Mama and she turned around. At first she didn't know what to do. It was a shock, imagine!

Then they both grabbed me and held me in their arms. They looked at my wrists, my wrists that still bore the marks of the handcuffs. And my mother started shouting: Look at what they did to you, those filthy beasts! They should die like snakes! They should pay for this! And my father trying to calm her down, telling her: But look, Mama, she's here. We've got her back. Calm down.

Each doing what came naturally. And right away I began to tell them: they did this to me . . . they did that. Telling my story, no? And I remember that I got to a certain point, talking about the torture, and suddenly my father turned to a friend who was with me and asked—it was a total non sequitur—do you know where your last name comes from?

He always liked that sort of thing, the roots of words, where names come from, their origins and so forth. And he just turned from what I was saying and began talking about her name. It was his way of saying: I can't listen to any more of this. His way of disconnecting. He couldn't stand it.

My years in exile were also terribly hard on my father. For my mother it was always about making sure we didn't need anything, she would send us whatever might make our lives easier. Because we were in Nicaragua for eight years, and you know the kind of scandal that went on here in Honduras with regard to Nicaragua: they don't have this, they don't have that. . . .

For the first year and a bit I couldn't make contact with my parents. For their safety and my own. But once I could be in touch, my mother would call us and ask: what do you need, what can I send you? And she'd spend her time getting things and sending them to us. I was in

Nicaragua for eight years, from 1982—just after my disappearance—
to 1990.

Because I knew Nora had met her husband while in exile in Nicaragua, I
wanted to know about their relationship, how it began, how it developed.

Yes, we met in exile. Shortly after I got to Nicaragua. And both of us being from Honduras, we naturally talked about our country, the places
or people we knew, things like that. But we were careful. We had to be.
He'd talk about the university, for instance, and I'd think to myself:
hmmm, this man taught at the university. But I didn't ask him outright.
The way he expressed himself, I don't know, I got the impression he'd
taught at the university. And I turned out to be right. In time we got
closer, we spent more time together, and fell in love.

I couldn't reveal too much about myself either. I remember we were
out in the country one afternoon, sitting under a tree, both of us reading. All of a sudden he said: I heard about this woman back home who
was kidnapped, her name is Nora Miselem. He was talking about my
experience, with pain in his voice, not knowing it was me. Nora Miselem, I said—it was a shock for me to be hearing my real name—that
sounds familiar. We'd talk like that. One of us would hear about something that had happened in our country, someone who had been imprisoned or murdered, and we'd talk about it. I don't think he had the
faintest idea he was talking about me.

Of course we had to clarify our identities with one another before we
returned to Honduras. Just before we left Nicaragua, he and I went together—and I was terrified, I can tell you—to the Honduran embassy
to register our children's births. Both children were born in Nicaragua.

We had to obtain documentation from a lawyer, and I found someone who didn't know who I was to draw up the papers for us. I had been
concerned, in any case, what if something happened to either or both
of us there in Nicaragua, what would happen to our children? That's
why I wanted to make sure that the children were legally registered,
not only in Nicaragua but in Honduras as well, where our families were.

Remembering now, it's almost funny. Legally speaking, our children's birth records had been a disaster. One of them appeared as if she were the daughter of a woman from the Soviet Union. I don't even know if it was me, in the midst of the labor pains, inventing who knows what sort of story—or if the officials just didn't understand what I said.

Once I got their birth certificates straightened out, I went to this lawyer and had a power of attorney drawn up, authorizing my mother to legally take the children out of Nicaragua in the event something happened to us. And it was in the context of all of this that I had to tell my husband my real name.

After the elections of 1990, when the Sandinistas lost, we all knew it was just a matter of time before the counterrevolutionaries—Nicaraguan and from other countries as well—would wreak havoc there. Under those conditions, I figured, I'm just as safe in Honduras. So I decided to come home.

And you know, each of us learning who the other was: it happened over a period of time. How to explain those times? By then my mother had come to visit on a number of occasions. And someone sent us a cassette addressed to me, and Renato listened to it. It started out: Nora . . . because this friend called me Nora. By the way, later on this friend was murdered here. She suffered horribly, they beat her to death: a writer, a poet who was quite well known, Clementina Suárez was her name. Anyway, she sent me this cassette, and she called me Nora all the way through it.

Then when my mother visited she too called me Nora once or twice, without thinking. So it was inevitable. Eventually we simply decided to clear up the matter of our names, at least with one another. But not with the children. And this created problems for them. When my son was born, for example, some Spaniards we knew began calling him Coco Liso, as an endearment: Baldy! And the Coco part of it stuck. So when he went to school they were still calling him Coco. But a psychologist I consulted at one point said he might have problems with that as he grew older. Because Coco really isn't a name.

When I was two and a half months pregnant with our son, my husband and I had to separate—for political reasons. He was sure it was going to be a boy—he was always sure of our children's sex, with the girl as well—and he told me, almost crying: When he's born please name him Leonardo. Because his name is Renato but he's a Leo. And he wanted me to name our son after him. But I didn't.

Anyway, I've gotten off the subject again. When my husband and I were getting ready to leave Nicaragua and return to Honduras, getting the children's papers in order and all that, that's when we really talked about our names, cleared that up with one another. But not with the children, no. They didn't know that their mother was Nora, either one of our names, until we were all back here and thoroughly settled in. For a long time, whenever somebody would call me Nora, my daughter would laugh. No, she would say, my mother's name is María.

I learned my husband's real name around the same time he learned mine. When it became absolutely necessary. We were getting ready to come back to Honduras. He dropped me off at the border, on the Nicaraguan side. And some members of my family—people we trusted completely—came to pick me up on the Honduran side. My husband dropped me off in a borrowed car, we didn't dare use our own car for that, and my family was waiting for me over here. There were plenty of witnesses, in case something happened.

The only thing that happened was the border guards asked for money. They made me pay an exorbitant fee to bring my children across; there was nothing we could do about that. I stood there, head held high, and I knew my family was on the other side. I could see that the official was trembling, and for a moment I wondered what might be about to happen. But it was only because he knew he was robbing me. He demanded a certain amount for each of the children. I gave him the dollars and that was that.

As I said, my husband dropped me off. He wanted to come with me, but at that point he actually had a more complicated situation than I did, because he had spent a number of years in Costa Rica before going on to Nicaragua. We had to say goodbye at that border as if we didn't know one another, as if he were a chauffeur who had brought me that far. Our farewell was: Do I still owe you something? I thought I paid you. Of course we knew we were surrounded by informants. The border is always full of them — *orejas* (ears) we call those guys who inform for the government. So I just said: No, I don't think I owe you anything.

Several days later he showed up here in Honduras. The same as with me, we made certain that family, people we trusted, met him and accompanied him the whole way.

I asked Nora how that transition was, from ten years of exile back to a country that may by then have seemed strange, or unfamiliar. I wanted to know what sorts of problems accompanied this family's reintroduction into Honduran society.

Well, for a long time our telephone was tapped. And then of course we had to live with my parents for quite a while. We had to depend on my family, economically, for much too long. Earning a living was really the hardest. It was easier for my husband than for me. He began teaching again at the university. It took him a while to get a regular position, and they paid him a miserable wage, the same salary he'd been earning when he'd left fifteen years before. It took them six months to begin paying him at all. But he got started in his profession again pretty soon after we returned.

For me it was more difficult. I'd been used to working hard, day and night, and I couldn't find anything here at all. I began to feel as if I was getting bogged down, not just in the sense of being able to earn a living but emotionally as well. I began to feel really bad. I did things here and there, attended to my father — which was important for me — but I needed a real job to be able to help support my family, to not feel like someone getting a free ride.

And it wasn't even just about the money, not really. Because I had never worked for money, never. I'd never been paid a salary for what I did. I started asking around, calling people, following one lead after another. But people . . . what can I say? People were afraid to have anything to do with me, that's the truth of it. I'd just come from Nicaragua, from all those years in exile. I knew people were afraid.

I even told them I don't care about the money. Just put me to work. Sweeping floors — anything to be able to feel useful. But I never heard back from anyone. No one called. Until finally, near the end of 1991, someone my husband ran into—he saw him on the street and gave him a ride and they started talking—this person asked what he was doing here, and he told him about Nicaragua, about my situation, the whole story.

My husband said he was here with his wife and two children, and this guy asked: Who is your wife? Nora Miselem, my husband replied. And it turned out the man had been a professor of mine at the university. So he recommended a couple of possibilities, and that's when I was able to get my first job after coming home. I was supposed to collect information on a particular topic, I can't even remember how much time they gave me to turn in the first collection of data, but neurotic that I am I worked day and night, and of course I turned in more and much sooner than they expected.

That first project had to do with the process our people went through in the transition from war to peace; I was supposed to interview members of the different political parties, right to left, and people from the Church, with regard to the implementation of the peace process. At last I felt useful and happy. And I worked all the time, day and night like I said.

This was a private institution, a women's organization that was mainly devoted to research. After that first project, these same people told me they wanted my help with a study on adoption in Honduras. I suggested they change the name of the study to Adoption: The Sale of Children in Honduras. This was basically an analysis of what came out in the newspapers about adoption, the sale of children, and so forth. Renato helped me a lot with that one, going through the daily papers for me and so forth.

They talk about adoption in this country because that's a way of referring to the legal part. But there are thousands of mothers here who are coerced into giving up their children for a pittance, and they are then sold for much higher prices; the middlemen are the ones who make the profit.

A lot of these children end up outside the country. Then it's the lawyers who profit, make huge sums of money. Sometimes they too are involved in the coercion, or outright thievery. Or they get women—because there are women who work in this as well—to convince other women—maybe a mother who has a number of children and can't support them all—they convince those mothers to sell their children, for nothing.

They even deal in specific ages. For example, they might tell someone: get me a three-year-old, as if they were speaking about an inanimate object of some kind. Get me a three-year-old. And they'll offer the person two thousand lempiras—$150 at the current rate of exchange. Almost nothing. And the money isn't even the worst of it. The worst is the fact that they tell someone: Get me a child. . . .

Well, I completed that study, and then the organization decided to hire m·full time. They brought me in to work in their documentation section—clipping newspapers, that sort of thing. And every once in a while I had the opportunity of working on a research project.

One of those projects ended up being very difficult for me, a very painful experience. Because it had to do with violence against young women in Honduras. I had to go to the forensic office, to investigate the most horrendous cases of death from battery or rape. Sexual abuse. And of course the work brought up my own experience of torture. I began to relive my own experience.

It was a horrible thing, and it turned me into an extremely aggressive person. I'd have to go over each case, and it was as if I were living it myself. I became the protagonist. The information you are given allows you to imagine the life of that particular young woman—her age, her family, how she suffered, the whole thing.

I'd be working on one of those cases and I'd find myself getting up from my chair, walking around, moving frenetically. And I wanted to tear off my clothing. I experienced the same burning sensation—especially in my vagina—as I had during the torture. I even bled, Margaret. I bled!

This is where I hoped Nora would be able to explore her experience more deeply. During our initial interview, the three of us had touched on the phenomenon of body memory. We'd talked about how the human body—

in this case a woman's body—remembers what has been done to it, even when the conscious mind may not. Fear, a sense of extreme impotence, and other emotions may cause a person to dissociate during the abuse, or to forget it later. Psychologists today understand that memories are quite literally stored in our cells. Subsequent experiences—the sound of a voice, a word, an image, even a scent—may awaken a body memory, uncovering episodes long forgotten.

I remembered that in our first conversation Nora had referred to her own body as an archive, a reference I'd found especially interesting, and I asked her to expand on that now.

In my case, memories of experiences too horrible to evoke with words or in images seem to live on in me in the form of pure pain. I think the body responds to our memories, even of other lives, through feelings, sensations, and the like. And I have the sense that we literally file these feelings, these sensations, away, in different parts of our body. So when we women hear other women tell their stories—and all our stories are so similar!—our body naturally makes the association.

When we first talked, I spoke of the body as an archive. Sometimes I think I would like to be able to work with my own archive. I wish we had therapists here in Honduras who specialized in that type of work. If I had the opportunity, I might be able to go into myself and process some of the pain. But for now, I believe the way we can best examine and process those experiences is through the struggle itself. All the time, every day. It is through our struggle to make a better world that we are able to work through the body memories. This is the only way we women have for breaking the chain of abuse. Otherwise it becomes pure repetition: the same thing, day after day.

But the other thing is that I believe we have to take a long hard look at the impunity, at the acceptance of violence against women in our society. It's simply accepted as something natural, something that cannot be changed. And that also makes for the repetition I'm talking about. It's always the same, the same. Every single story you hear. It might be an indigenous woman rebelling against her situation. Or a woman living in a rural area. It's always the same.

It's as if our system of justice just cannot move past that. I think that to the degree we women are able to break with the conventional acceptance of that violence, to the degree that we are able to break with traditional values and tell our stories, to that precise degree we will be able to liberate everyone. But it's not easy; it's such a difficult struggle.

Nora lit a fresh cigarette with the one she had been smoking. Her eyes seemed to pool browner and deeper as she spoke about the weight of struggle. I thought of the case she had started to build when we met in Managua, the effort to bring her own experience to light, to be able to name the guilty and hold them in some way accountable. It had been October when we first spoke of this. Now it was April. I asked how it was going.

The struggle continues, and the situation is basically the same as it was then. Some days are better than others. I find myself feeling hopeful one day and hopeless the next. And I think there are objective reasons for that. The very slowness with which everything progresses here. It's been six months, and nothing has really happened! How should I feel about that? And how can I process what I'm feeling inside? That's the main thing. Having decided to take my case to court hasn't helped with the physical pain. And then there's the emotional pain, which is much greater than its physical counterpart. I'm so tired of all this, and that in and of itself is painful.

Of course I'm not in this alone. When the Public Ministry decided to take this on, and they opened a special human rights office to receive our accusations, I heard about it from several people, and they all urged me to present my case. Immediately . . . oh, I had such hope at the beginning! I thought the moment had finally come when I would be able to act, to do something. . . . I wanted so badly to be able to pay life back for having survived. Like this might finally be the moment to be able to do something for the dead, for all those who perished, who didn't come back.

I asked Nora if she sees this process as being primarily for them, for those who didn't come back. Or if she is also doing it for herself.

Oh, I'm doing it for them. Yes, I believe that's the most important thing. So few of us, men or women, survived. So few, and I think it's the least we can do for those who didn't. We few who returned are the living proof of what happened to the others. The proof of how they died.

What can I say? When I heard about the possibility of taking my case to court, I began talking to people, others who had also suffered torture or been kidnapped. . . . I got in touch with Father Fausto Milla in the western part of the country, and he came right away. Because he had also been victimized during those years. And I spoke with others, people I knew who like me had suffered repression back then. We all went to give our initial testimonies to the authorities set up to receive them.

One thing that did strike me then was that in some of these cases, they were very careful to take down all the information: names, events, dates, etc. They told us that this was basically a formality, no? But in my case I didn't see that they took much note of what I said, no. They listened, I told them what I'd gone through, but that was it. And then the waiting began. And I waited, hopeful at times, hopeless at others. I wondered when they would call me back, so that I could make my formal protest before the proper authorities. Finally they did call me, after quite a long time had passed, and then they took note of everything.

But, you know, several months had passed. At least. Enough so that I despaired of anything really happening. I guess they were setting up the ministry, though. It was a complex process: not only the human rights section but the section on corruption, another on women, children, and so forth . . . one must be fair.

But I kept waiting. And waiting. And I wasn't idle during that time. I was busy looking for possible witnesses, people who could testify to having seen me when I came out of those prisons. And the officials also called a number of witnesses. We had to find people, others who had suffered as well. We did all this, but then the case changed hands— another special prosecutor came on board. And this is a person who has a certain commitment to human rights.

But, you know, it's not about a single person, whether or not that person is committed to some semblance of justice. It's also about the resources to which they have access. And I think the efforts these people have made have been very disperse; they haven't received the support they need within the system. A great deal of investigation is needed in order to truly substantiate our cases. All sorts of resources are needed: human resources, funding, time. And I don't see any of that really happening.

Well, the same system is still in place. The system that existed when all these crimes were committed. Even some of the same people. And so of course there's fear as well. Because there have been times when . . . for a while now, several months, I don't see anything happening. Not really. There has been some activity. Maybe some things have happened, but very slowly. And then, in the last few months, there's been no activity. Or none that I can see. Maybe one of the main obstacles has been the judicial system itself. Of what are these people going to be accused? What are the crimes, what do we call them? There are crimes that are not even contemplated within our statutes. And there are others for which they do have names but for which the statute of limitations has run out.

For example, kidnapping or forced disappearance, which is the name they use, has never been contemplated within the judicial system here. Even if they succeed in adding it to the penal code, they may not be able to do so retroactively. And that's the essential thing in a case like mine. They may be able to add kidnapping or disappearance to the list of crimes in this country, but in so doing they may be making sure that justice is not served in a crime like the one perpetrated against me, because fifteen years have gone by.

By adding kidnapping or forced disappearance to the list, they can make it a crime today, or in the future. And this also serves to take the pressure off them. Because there's been an increase in this sort of crime by bands of common criminals that are active today. I'm not saying it wouldn't be useful in those cases. But it ought to be retroactive as well.

Of course the crimes today are of a delinquent nature. Before they were political. The nature of the crime is different, but the crime itself is similar. Cases like mine seem to fall into a legal void, I don't know. What else can I tell you? Well, these are really the main things, the obstacles we've faced: the lack of resources and the poverty of a legal system that doesn't even contemplate cases like ours as crimes.

I thought for a moment about the obstacles faced by anyone attempting to get the most minimal satisfaction in a situation like Nora's. I thought about the processes that have taken place in other countries, where so many emerged revictimized. Power, by its very nature, defies accountability. I knew that the struggle being waged by Nora and others like her was not likely to produce the results she hoped for. Certainly not in the legal or penal arenas. To put it bluntly, the guilty were not likely to be punished. Becoming involved in this new battle and reliving the horrors it would inevitably bring up was risky at best. It meant months, maybe years, of revisiting her torture with only the slimmest possibility of what most people would consider victory. Perhaps it did have to be enough to be doing this for the dead, for those who hadn't survived, whose voices had been silenced. But I couldn't help hoping that in some hidden recess of her psyche Nora might also be doing this for herself. That going through this process might give her some closure, some degree of personal resolution.

I think my internal reasons for doing this have to do with . . . no, I know this is true: I simply cannot separate myself from those others who fought and were tortured to death or murdered, those who didn't return. That's my main reason for doing this. And that was always my cause.

One of the things this special office is trying to establish is the crime of intent to murder. It's very difficult to prove, of course. But we need to be able to establish why we were released. The guilty can say they acted in good faith, simply because they released us, because they didn't end up murdering us. If they'd wanted to murder us, they would have. That's their position.

So we have to be able to show that there was international pressure in our case. And I have to be able to show that even after I was free they continued to harass and persecute me. It's difficult. But, what can I tell you? One of the main reasons I've decided to go through with this is that it's not only about winning. After all, what does it mean to win a case like this one, really? Are we hoping for a sentence? I don't think it makes much difference, at this point, if the people who perpetrated the crimes against me are given a year or ten years. What I'm looking for is the truth. Not a sentence, necessarily, just the truth.

I want the guilty to accept responsibility for what they did. I want to bring attention to them, so that people will know who they are, what they did. If nothing else, I would like my case to expose some of the higher-ups, so that people will hear their side of the story, the reasons they may have had for acting as they did, and that all this may serve to clarify as well the cases of those who did not return. I've often said: I'm alive, I survived, I came back. I don't want the guilty punished for me but for the others.

I know the damage done to me. And I know that many others suffered much greater damage. And with less resources than I've had to be able to survive the aftereffects. It's not an easy experience to survive—the captivity, the torture, and then what you live with year after year, minute after minute. It's not easy.

What helps most is the sense of dignity we retain as human beings. And the fact that we were conscious, from the beginning, that it wouldn't be easy, that we might easily lose our lives in the struggle. I never expected to come out alive. I've told you that.

Yes. I remember your saying that in October. I remember how struck I was by the fact that you didn't expect to survive and that María never believed she would die. I found that interesting, how differently each of you felt about what the outcome of your ordeal would be. Maybe because you lived here, you knew firsthand what your country's security forces and paramilitary operatives were capable of. Or maybe because María was from another country, she thought that might go in her favor ultimately. Although, really, I believe that the fact that each of you were sure it would end differently responds as well to something deeper . . . your different natures perhaps.

Nora, I want to ask you a question that seems very important to me. It's a question that's important to me personally, and one that I believe is important for all of us who during those years, in whatever spot on earth we were involved, were working for a more just society. We saw the Cuban Revolution, the socialist revolutions in different places, to a certain extent even the revolution in the Soviet Union, as emblematic of that just society for which we fought. Oh, there were problems, things with which we didn't agree. But we looked to those experiments as proof of the possibility that society might be organized differently, with justice for more of its members.

Many of us have come to believe that we were betrayed in our struggles, betrayed in two essential ways. I don't know if you agree with this. In spite of the fact that the Cuban Revolution lives—and remains a beacon of hope for so many—very few of those experiences are intact today. There are a few countries that continue to call themselves socialist, but they have little to do with the visions we had then.

We are of a generation, to a greater or lesser extent depending on who and where we are, that has suffered tremendous loss. Human loss as well as the loss of an ideal. Many of us feel a bitterness, against parties and organizations, perhaps even against ourselves. And we women, within that overall picture, also suffer a particular sense of betrayal. So many of us worked hard, sacrificed a great deal, gave years of our lives, or gave our whole lives, and were to an extent betrayed.

I don't know if you would use the word betrayal. I use it with deliberate intention. But whether or not you would use that word, I believe you know what I'm talking about: that as women we were never really taken into account, we never achieved the positions of power that might have allowed our own visions to prosper. There wasn't any real gender equality, even in struggles that insisted they were being waged to bring about equality for everyone.

Nevertheless, here we are, those of us who survived. And many of us continue in the same struggles. You are certainly one who does. Despite all this, we continue to believe in the vision of justice to which we gave so much. And we continue the work, each in her particular area. But a number of women, in a number of different countries, have left the mixed political parties. We didn't find the space or respect we needed in those organizations. Some of us have joined with other feminists in an attempt to create *new forms of struggle and with a vision that analyzes power and is more inclusive of all the different social groups.*

Most of us are feminists with roots in the struggle for social change. In this we differ from our feminist sisters who have roots in the women's movement per se. How do you see all this? I guess my first question would be: Do you agree with what I've just outlined? Has this been your experience as well? And then, if it has, how do you see your struggle today, what work are you currently involved in, as a woman who wants a society of justice for all? It's a different Honduras now, one in which the old terror is not so rampant, but it's certainly not a just society. And we also live in a different world now—in which our enemies have much more power than they did in the 1970s and 1980s. How do you see your own life of struggle, particularly your life as a woman, within the context of your country today, and within the context of today's world?

Look, if we're going to talk about betrayal, we have to understand that we were betrayed by men and also by women. It wasn't our cause, our dream, our utopia that failed us. And these remain alive for me today. Those of us who made mistakes, who worked in the wrong way, we failed. And I blame those most of all who worked in the wrong way and were conscious of doing so. Some of us made innocent mistakes; others knew what they were doing—those who abused their positions of power, who wouldn't permit the same sort of democratization inside the different organizations as they claimed to be fighting for in society as a whole.

That greater democratization would have made for a greater participation on the part of women. But I'm not complaining about that. What did our men do, after all, that we didn't do? Nothing. I believe that our participation, as women, was vital, total. What's more, I think women's participation gives soul to the struggle.

I know we women didn't make the decisions. In the main we didn't have that power. But I ask myself, did we really try to win that battle? I'm sure each experience has been different, but I know from my own that there were those of us who conformed to the norm, who accepted our roles—what's more, we didn't even notice! We didn't question the status quo, we didn't perceive of ourselves as secondary or bother to fight for more power.

Maybe a few of us did. Some few of us did have clarity around these issues. And our struggle wasn't easy. We waged it, and we lost. Some of us did fight for greater democratization, a different order, within our organizations. That's what I mean when I say that we women bring soul to struggle, or try to. And if we didn't succeed overall, we did succeed in certain instances.

Our history is a complex one. There are particular experiences; we just can't generalize. Our struggle has faces. Faces of women, of men, of girls and boys, young people, old people, even very old people. And we women see those faces. And then, the system has always demanded that women be there for others rather than for ourselves. I think it's important to look to the soul of all this, the subjective aspect, the feelings. Feelings are so much a part of women's identity. We cannot separate them out.

Nora paused, lit another cigarette, and fell silent for a time. I asked her to tell me something about how the struggle in Honduras looks today. What those involved in trying to change society are doing, what some of the battles are. Nora emitted a long sigh before continuing to speak.

Everyone has her or his own idea of how to struggle, I think. There are those who have simply adjusted to the way things are; they think those of us who are still involved in social or political activism are crazy, that we're living a tired dream. Others have accommodated themselves in positions of power; they don't even think about the struggle any more.

But I believe that everyone must hold onto her or his utopian dream. I don't care if we call it communism, or by another name. Certainly we need a different kind of society, one in which people have the right to life, to jobs, to security, health. That need for change remains valid. I don't care what name we give it. As long as it's a place of justice for all of us, women and men. That's the bottom line.

So I believe that the dreams we had, the cause for which we fought, continues to be valid. Isn't it true that the world is more divided every day? And every day there are fewer there at the top, fewer who reap the profits of the work the rest of us do. Every day there are fewer bosses and more masses of people without even minimal rights. I can't understand how people can question what we wanted, I can't!

The problem today, as I see it, is that the owner class has developed such sophisticated mechanisms by which to keep us down that we do their work for them; we are killing one another among ourselves. We're saving them the trouble! Here in Honduras I see that we women— with all the violence that's generated against us—we're afraid to go out into the streets. We seem to be afraid of everything!

And we don't have what you'd call a feminist movement, or strong feminist organizations. One of the problems we still have here is how we define the term *feminist*. It's all much too simplistic. For example, if you're in favor of abortion, you're considered a feminist. If you're not, no. And abortion continues to be completely illegal in Honduras, even in a case of rape. It doesn't matter if you've been raped, if you'll die giving birth, nothing. Abortion is completely against the law.

This is such a widespread problem, and yet it's not easy to even talk about it in Honduras. It's a subject we have to approach with utmost care. A person who comes out in favor of abortion here simply disgraces her or himself. No. No way. Margaret, there's such a double morality in this country, and it's so deeply ingrained in our social fabric . . . in spite of the fact that abortion exists here. Abortion exists. Without talking about it. Abortion, after all, is not a feminist invention. Abortion has existed from time immemorial. As in many places, there are doctors who practice abortion, and there are women who are able to have one if they need to. But you need money. Who are those who die for lack of legal abortion? The poor, of course.

And we've just recently seen reforms in our penal code, reforms that make it much more difficult, much riskier to perform an abortion— for the doctor, for anyone caught aiding or abetting . . . severe penalties. At the same time, those in power here continue to say no to condoms, no to any sort of contraceptive device.

There's a great deal of attack against those who discuss family planning. The pro-life people, Opus Dei, the whole Catholic hierarchy—

of course there are also sectors of the Church with a very different mentality, much more open-minded about these things—but the Church hierarchy here in Honduras is diametrically opposed to the use of condoms.

Where I work, the Women's Human Rights Organization, we've been doing some educational outreach via regular radio programs and the like, and we've been working on the issue of reproductive rights in particular. But we have a terrible struggle on our hands. There's so much adverse propaganda, from the Church, from all sorts of places: about condoms not working, about people dying even when they use condoms, discouraging their use by any means.

This propaganda screams out about promiscuity; it tells young women that all they need to do is be faithful. Sure! It's fine to be faithful, but what about our men? In a society like ours it's the men we have to worry about. Women need to have the right to protect themselves. We are trying to put forth the idea that each of us must take responsibility for our own life. I can't be responsible for my husband if I know he's the one who's being promiscuous!

Who are those who have AIDS in this country? Our housewives are getting the disease, not our prostitutes or our sex workers as they're called—which is what people want to believe. Our homosexuals aren't the ones with AIDS, no. The largest "group" of people with AIDS here in Honduras is the group composed of housewives, women whose promiscuous husbands have given them the disease. They are the ones who are dying of AIDS, because of their husbands' irresponsible attitudes and conduct.

And if condoms aren't 100 percent safe, if out of every hundred, say ten may fail, well at least ninety users would be protected. We cannot responsibly continue to say no to condoms. And this is the campaign that is raging here today, on the part of the Church, Opus Dei, the pro-life groups, and so forth.

Our organization mounts a countercampaign of course. Even the Ministry of Health has its countercampaign. But there's a real war going on against these countercampaigns. And you know, at times we are even in the position of having to join forces with some of those

U.S.-backed organizations, like USAID. We have to agree with their campaigns. Perhaps not for the same reasons, but we find ourselves on the same side of many of these issues.

We aren't advocating for contraception or birth control in order to avoid the demographic explosions some other countries have experienced; we're advocating for the lives of women, for their rights, for the quality of life that women deserve. We defend a woman's right to decide about her body. Because the truth is, we have our children and it's generally the husband who decides when we become pregnant, and there isn't even any equality here in terms of parental responsibility.

Here in Honduras they don't go after men to force them to assume responsibility for their offspring; it's women they accuse of negligence, of being bad mothers. We women are obliged to care for our children. And we have been trying to get sex education into our schools, from the earliest grades. But that too is an uphill battle.

In a very few schools they try to talk about some things. And, I'm telling you, it's not only the Church that reacts when this happens; it's also the parents. A great many parents object to their children being told about anything sexual. It's incredible how many parents complain if their children hear anything at all about sex at school.

So, to get back to your question about women, and about the sorts of struggles that exist here, I would say there is a feminist movement here, albeit incipient with respect to some of the other Central American countries. There are certainly those of us who call ourselves feminists, who demand the right to call ourselves that. I wouldn't say that we're very advanced. We're just learning, beginning, growing. And there are women here who don't call themselves feminists—what's more, they would be insulted by the term—but nevertheless are feminists, understand? They are feminist by virtue of their struggles.

The thing is, the power structure here has made it a point to discredit the term *feminist*. If you're a feminist, you're a lesbian, they say. If you're a feminist, you necessarily agree with abortion. If you're a feminist, well, it means that you identify with a whole series of issues that many women reject. And a great many women believe this sort of propaganda; it affects them. So they might say: well, I'm a feminist but I'm not a radical one. Or: no, I'm not a feminist, I'm just fighting for women's rights. These women might even be radical, in the context of what our society is, but they still claim not to be feminists.

Is there a lesbian community here in Tegucigalpa? I know there are lesbians, but is there any sort of community? I'm not speaking geographically, of course, but I'm interested in knowing if there are places—bars or cafés for example—where lesbians gather. Or a magazine or an organization of some sort?

I'm going to tell you something. I know only one lesbian here in Tegucigalpa, and it's not that we've talked about her sexual identity, nothing like that. But people know, basically because she's come out in some of the international forums where lesbians from other countries also are. Here, not on your life!

I have talked with other women about this; I've said that we need to be dealing with this reality. I've advocated for opening up the discussion, dealing with the fact that there are lesbians among us and that they have nowhere to go, no place to address their issues. Lesbians here must endure such aggression—you have no idea! If they reveal themselves, they are automatically thought of as worthless.

I can honestly tell you that the organization I work for is among the most advanced there is in terms of discussing all sorts of women's issues, and we simply have not addressed this one, never. Even in our radio shows, we've touched on all sorts of subjects: family planning, infidelity—which is another taboo—but never homosexuality.

One of the reasons I asked this question is that this morning, when I got up, you were still asleep, and I came downstairs to read a bit. I found a small book of poetry on your dining room table, and I glanced through it. The book was dedicated to your children, and it was written by a woman called Juana La Loca (Juana, the Crazy One). And I noticed a poem about lesbianism that made me think that the poet is a lesbian, or woman-identified. Is this a poet who is considered important here?

Juana is a poet. She's a person who's come on strong with regard to the nation's sacred cows, important political figures, the hierarchy of the Catholic Church, and so forth. She's ferocious when it comes to defending her ideas, or how she wants to live her life. And she's written a lot about women's lives, rich women, poor women, prostitutes and saints. Juana doesn't forget what women go through, and she writes about a broad range of conditions and options. In her poems she is Everywoman, because she wants to show that there is no single model or type of woman but rather that each and every one of us is unique, that there's no such thing as women as a group but rather that women are part of every social group: Indians, mestizos, rich, poor, prostitutes, saints, and so forth.

Juana is as likely to drink in the homes of the rich as she is with winos in the street. She'll fight with the cops and anyone else in defense of her ideas. One of her themes is live and let live. I admire her lack of respect for all that reeks of power, or is power, especially patriarchy. Juana Pavón, or Juana La Loca has been willing to speak out about those subjects no one else is willing to touch. So she speaks openly and directly about lesbianism as she does about any other condition or right of women. Most people don't take her seriously; they don't dare.

It's interesting that an out-and-out feminist position is still so taboo in Honduras. Because in some of the other Central American countries, in Nicaragua, for example, and in Costa Rica, there are strong independent feminist movements, including lesbians who are organized. And these feminist movements have strong roots in social struggle. Even in Cuba there is beginning to be an independent feminist movement, separate from the Federation of Cuban Women (FMC), which is the official women's organization within the revolutionary structure. And many of these independent feminists in Cuba are longtime revolutionaries—many of them are members of the Cuban Communist Party—yet they understand the need for independent feminist organizing.

For example, there's a group called MAGIN . . . a group of women who work as journalists in the different media, in television, radio, the written press. They've been organizing for several years now, around issues not so much of women's rights—which are covered, at least in a general way, within the revolution—but of how women are portrayed in the media, what erroneous concepts and images of women still persist in Cuba despite more than four decades of revolution. These women have been developing a gender analysis of Cuban society, and they touch on issues such as power, sexist language, sexist images of women, and so forth.

But you know, Nora—and this goes back to what I was trying to get at before when I asked you about women who have been members of mixed organizations, if they've felt any bitterness toward those organizations' failure to address women's issues—a few years ago the Cuban Communist Party refused to recognize MAGIN, refused to accord it status as a nongovernmental organization. In Cuba this is tantamount to putting it out of existence. It's the power the old-timers at the Federation of Cuban Women still hold, and their fear when an independent group emerges.

What have the members of MAGIN done in response to that?

As Party members—many of the founders are—they simply decided to accept the dictate of their Party for now. In any case, I don't think this is the end of MAGIN. They have sown powerful seeds, which aren't going to wither or die just because they cannot organize at this time. But I think it's a sad mistake on the part of the Cuban Communist Party not to be able to recognize and acknowledge difference, the need for more than one group. Fear of feminism is widespread.

It's so difficult. So difficult.

Nora, I'd like to ask you about your personal relationship with your husband who is also your comrade.[1] I have felt a tremendous sense of harmony in your home. Your husband has been away during the time I've been here, but I can tell that it's a home with harmony, and that the harmony transcends the fact of his immediate presence. It was one of the first things I noticed when I arrived: the feeling of harmony with your children, in the house in general. I tend to sense these things, to feel them.

And I wanted to ask you—I'm not sure if you'll be able to answer this, or even if you'll want to—but I'd like to know if the tortures that you suffered when you were disappeared—specifically the sexual torture, the rape, the sexual damage, the affronts to your dignity as a woman—I'd like to know if your husband has been able to help you deal with the scars those tortures must have left, if he's been able to help you with that? Maybe I should ask you first if there are scars. I'm assuming that there are, there have to be . . .

Of course there are. You know how he helps me? Sometimes I'm amazed at his patience. When he wants to make love, sometimes we're together, feeling intimate, all the conditions are right, and suddenly I just can't continue. And not only because I believe that I have the right to claim what my body needs at any given moment—I'm certainly not one of those women who thinks she has to please her husband any time he wants. But when I too want to make love, when I too desire that and suddenly just can't, his patience has been exemplary.

There was a time when I was even more affected by the aftermath of the torture than I am now. I suffered terrible pains, physical pains. . . . It's been fifteen years and I still have pain. It's gotten a lot better since I had an operation to lift my uterus. Because there was the damage from the torture, and then it seems that damage was intensified by my subsequent deliveries, the births of my son and daughter. But getting back to my husband: he's always had a great deal of patience with me. In the very moment in which I might be rejecting him, he'll tell me: You don't know how much I love you.

He reminds me that he loves me, no matter what. It's his way of telling me that he understands what I've been through. And there's all the rest of it: his patience when, in the midst of such a terribly macho society, he is willing to share his life with me. In spite of the difficulties. There are times, Margaret, when I know my experience has made me a difficult person to live with.

Renato and I have gone through a lot together. At the beginning of our relationship I tended to want to be alone a lot. I needed to get away, flee if you will. I needed so much solitude. It was more about going inside myself, being away from people, including the man I loved. I know that lots of people have the need to go inside, to order their thoughts, to be alone once in a while. But in my case it wasn't just that. It was a choice to be alone in order to suffer my pain without anyone else around.

I remember, when we were together in Nicaragua, we had such a large house, I could simply have gone into another room. But I had to get away, be completely alone. And I'd go out into the garden, sit under a tree, and think—or feel. We shared everything, Renato and I, and I knew he would be looking for me, wondering where I was. But I had to be alone.

Sometimes he'd say he wished he could get inside what I feel. I'd told him about the tortures, from the beginning. And sometimes he'd say he wished he could get inside of me, to share what I'd been through. Of course he couldn't. And I continue to need that solitude, to be alone with my experience, to try to understand it perhaps. I don't deny myself that right, but I also know how hard it must be for him sometimes, for the life we want to make together.

I've often thought to myself, Renato deserves someone else, someone easier to be with than me. Sometimes I think I'm not fair to drag him along, to make him the victim of my own reactions: my sadness, my need for solitude. But I also think I've changed some. With the years, I've learned to be happier, much happier. I can joke again, that sort of thing.

And Renato has also changed. He was never a very lively person, never given to joking around. He was very serious. And he too has loosened up. We've been able to open to one another and to open up our own little world, to include more festivity, more joy.

Besides whatever therapy you've had—I know about your hospital stay, after the murder of your first child, and I assume you've had some therapy to help you deal with the experience of torture—have you ever been able to get together with other survivors of torture, women or men, to deal collectively with the experience? What I'm asking is, are there any groups here, opportunities for torture victims to get together and share their experiences and share possible ideas or techniques for healing?

And I ask this because in the United States, in the context of widespread childhood sexual abuse, incest, that sort of thing—which is different, of course, but also similar in many ways—victims have found it very useful to get together and help one another recover and survive. Women, especially, have organized ourselves in this way. And there are whole communities of people in recovery. I'm wondering if there's been the opportunity, or even the desire, to do something similar here?

With the center I mentioned before, when we've tried to deal with the rehabilitation of the torture victims, I've thought: how wonderful it would be to be able to talk with others who have experienced what I've gone through! How wonderful to be able to talk to one another, in our own words, express what we're feeling, so many years after the fact. The rage, the pain . . . We need common projects, for the future as well, to help us get strong again, to help us reclaim our energies, particularly when working with these cases.

I was so excited about the prospect of being able to talk to other victims, so excited. But it didn't happen. I approached them, and I was looking forward to group sessions and so forth. But nothing. Everything was handled with individual appointments, with a medical doctor, a lawyer, that sort of thing. I've heard about visualizations. There was this woman from the United States. She was going to give us lessons in visualization. And talk to us about acupressure as well. But it never happened.

I was able to attend a workshop once, a while back. This woman also had a method for having us visualize our experiences. There were a number of women present. And this woman, with her sweet voice, talked to us, urged us . . . and every one of those women were transported, if you will, every one of them went somewhere and visualized what they hoped to visualize.

Except me.

And you have to remember what my particular experience was. In the torture, I heard that same sort of voice, urging me, coercing me. So in that workshop, all I felt were reactions in my body: itching, whatever. I resisted by every means possible being taken in by that voice. I couldn't close my eyes. I couldn't go anywhere.

And I understood. In the torture I was forced to respond to voices— and I was blindfolded, I couldn't see—while they tortured me with electric shocks. How was I supposed to respond to this sort of technique? It was the same when they operated on me; I told the doctor: Put me out. I don't want to hear anyone's voice while I'm undergoing whatever it is I'm going to be undergoing. I just can't respond to that sort of thing, voices telling me to do this or that. I'm too resistant. So that's really not an option for me.

I wasn't thinking about that sort of mechanism: hypnotism, or anything like that. Those are useful techniques and they have their place, though perhaps not with people like yourself. I was thinking rather of a peer group, of people who had suffered similar experiences, just talking with one another.

I was thinking that there is a culture of torture, so to speak, a culture shared by the victims of torture, one that only those victims may be capable of inhabiting. And I was thinking that a group of such people, coming together without anyone else present, might be useful in terms of dealing with the aftereffects, the scars.

You'd speak the same language, a language perhaps no one else really knows. Perhaps you'd even share some of the same scars. And maybe one or another of you would be able to suggest an experience of healing that could be beneficial to the others. Sometimes just talking, among people who do share the same language, can be very important. I know that the Chileans have explored this route, and others too.

Yes I'm sure that would be useful. But unfortunately here in Honduras, I don't know. I really don't know why we haven't been able to do anything like that. Maybe there hasn't been enough trust among those affected. Maybe people are still afraid.

SIX

MARÍA

San José is as different from Tegucigalpa as West Hollywood from the ghettos of South Central Los Angeles. Costa Rica is the most modern of the Central American countries. It was in María's small but comfortable apartment—the tiny house in the countryside to which she would soon move wasn't finished yet—that I set up my tape recorder and prepared to interview this woman who usually situates herself on the other side of the microphone. I wanted to begin by exploring her life before the events of 1982. I wanted to know about her family of origin and what class and cultural experiences had led her to assume her political commitment. What events had brought her to the apartment from which she was disappeared.

My grandparents, on both sides, came from Spain. The photographs I have hanging there in the hall [two rows of framed portraits] are of the two lines of women, on both my father's and mother's sides, beginning with my great-great-grandmothers. You can see the Galician features in their faces. My paternal great-great-grandfather was a shoemaker in the Spanish army. His son came to this continent and did fairly well; I always say my grandparents were middle class. They weren't enormously wealthy, but neither did they have to live strictly on what they earned. My grandfather on my mother's side was a dentist. My paternal grandfather was the businessman from Galicia.

My father is an engineer, a civil engineer who lived from his profession but always resisted going to work for any of the large U.S. corporations. They never destroyed his spirit in that sense.

And my mother was a teacher. She's actually had three professions in her life, although it was as a ceramicist that she was able to contribute to the family economy. And more recently she's begun to write. My parents managed to educate all six of their children in private Catholic schools.

I'm the next to the oldest of my siblings, the oldest female, the second in a line of six, and Mom and Dad wanted to have seven. Mom, in fact, wanted only sons. That is something that has marked me, indelibly, throughout my life. Fortunately, it's also something I've been able to talk about with her. In any case, I'm the second in my family, the oldest of the girls. We are three girls and three boys.

We lived in a wealthy neighborhood, Villa Caparra [in Puerto Rico], on a street called Doctor Toro. The street bears my grandfather's name. When I was born it was pure countryside. My grandfather, the dentist, willed three pieces of land to his three children, one of them being my mother. It was countryside, as I say, rough and inhospitable. And far from the capital, San Juan.

My mother and father built their home and went to live out there. In time, the area became a well-to-do neighborhood, Los Blanquitos de Villa Caparra. It was a very elitist neighborhood and home to one of the most prestigious Catholic schools in Puerto Rico. So we were raised there, in that context, and we studied at that school. But somehow we never really fit in. Nor did we want to.

My parents were people who challenged the status quo. And they weren't social climbers. Because Puerto Rico is a colony of the United States, you have all sorts of possibilities—as well as lack of possibilities. But there are two categories that I think especially important: the people who are intent upon moving up in society and those who aren't. The very fact that my father, an engineer, was never interested in working for one of the big U.S. companies is indicative of the fact that he wasn't interested in moving up. My mother was also very resistant to upward mobility.

I wouldn't say she was terribly politicized, but she was resistant. She always taught us to be proud of being Puerto Rican. And although she let us know that there were times when we would have to compromise,

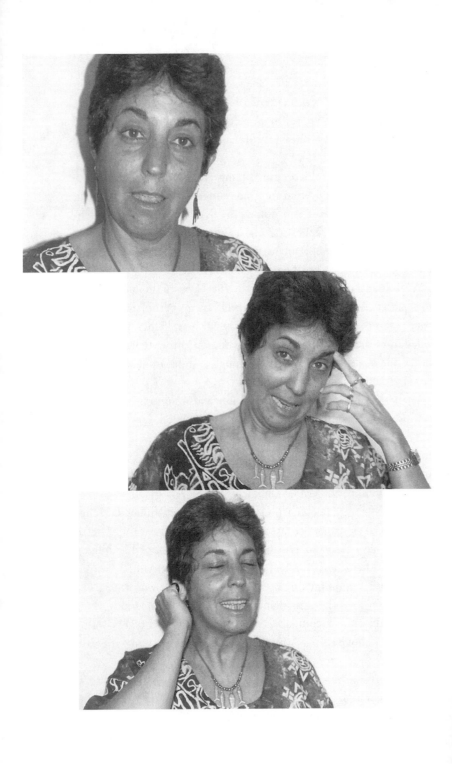

Portraits of María Suárez, taken by Margaret Randall during interviews also conducted by Randall, in San José, Costa Rica, in April 1997.

she wanted us to do it without losing sight of who we were, of our personalities, our spirit, our way of thinking. This is the way in which I conceptualize my mother's early politics.

Why Costa Rica? What brought you here?

I married a Costa Rican . . .

Wait a minute. You married a Costa Rican, but you divorced the Costa Rican. And yet you stayed.

Of course. It's not about the marriage. And it's an interesting question. I've asked myself that question on a number of occasions.

When I was studying in Albany, actually I was already working as a professor at the university by that time—I'm talking about 1970, 1971, 1972—I was teaching bilingual education, as a Puerto Rican, during the years when bilingual education was an extension . . . well, not an extension, but rather an expression on the part of Latin American men and women of our position in the U.S. civil rights struggle, the movement against the Vietnam War, the Black Panthers and all that.

At that time, within the general intensity of all those movements, there was what I'll call an identity struggle on the part of Latin American women and men inside the United States to forge and preserve our own identities. Not to mention our participation in the other struggles.

In this context I'd become very close to the Puerto Rican community in the United States—second generation, or first generation born in that country—and it was a community I didn't know, because I'd been born and raised in Puerto Rico. And I also felt a sense of belonging within the larger Latin American community. In Albany we were organized into an Association of Latin American Students. As such, we protested the war in Vietnam, we fought for our Latin American identity, and we talked about underdevelopment, dependency, and the various revolutions going on at the time.

For me, that group of Latin American women and men, including the Puerto Ricans—very few of whom even spoke Spanish, because they were so assimilated, and among whom I saw myself reflected, and also feared for whom I might become—that was the community in which I searched for my identity. Those students helped me redefine myself, grapple more deeply with my own issues, find my Latin American roots.

As a Puerto Rican living in Puerto Rico I'd been pretty isolated from those roots. Because blockades are not only economic in nature. Puerto Rico was never economically blockaded; on the contrary, it was the showcase of U.S. consumerism. But Puerto Rico has been blockaded politically, in terms of its identity and in terms of its relationship to other Latin American countries. And so, in that Latin American community inside the United States, I found an important part of my roots.

And I embarked on a relationship with one of those organized Latin American students, a Costa Rican, and we decided to come here to Costa Rica to live. I feel that in my marriage to this man—in spite of the fact that it was a marriage based on love, a relationship forged in the context of struggle—my need was basically that of reconnecting to Latin America. To come back and live where my roots were. The part of my roots that had previously been denied me. . . .

What I liked about Costa Rica, without really knowing the country . . . I mean, as a child I had visited several Latin American countries because I'd participated in swimming championships in different places, but that's another sort of knowing. I'd been to Mexico, Colombia, and El Salvador, and those visits had been very important for me. But when I came to Costa Rica with the man I was going to marry, what impressed me about the country, and what strengthened my decision to move here, was that back then—and I'm talking about 1972, 1973—Costa Rica felt like the Puerto Rico of my childhood. And that Puerto Rico of my childhood no longer existed.

The rhythm of life here was that of a small town or village, not the rhythm of a large city. People's spirit was less fearful, more loving. There was a feeling of safety in the streets. And an infinite vision of green. And there was an attitude about legality, about the way things were done, that allowed you to live more or less by your own rules, without excessive aggressiveness or corruption.

This was Costa Rica in the early seventies, very similar to the Puerto Rico of my childhood—which I yearned for still. Because in spite of the fact that I grew up in the neighborhood I described to you, in spite of the fact that I studied at an elitist Catholic school, both my parents were passionate fishing people. We were raised by the sea. We grew up in communities of fishermen and fisherwomen, in small fishing villages, for example, in the region of Loisa Aldea where the inhabitants are black, an almost closed community where people lived as they had for years.

So the Puerto Rico I had known—and I'd rejected elitist Puerto Rico—was effectively what I found when I came to Costa Rica. And I fell in love with this country. I fell in love with her people. Unfortunately, Costa Rica has now become Puertoriquenized, if you will. In just five years Costa Rica has gotten to the point that it took Puerto Rico eighteen or twenty-five years to get to. The everyday stress, the upward mobility, the corruption, the deterioration of people's standard of living, the whole thing: what we see today in terms of the social conditions that have been imposed.

But I came to Costa Rica back then to put down my Latin American roots, to retrieve my Latin American identity. Afterward I traveled to other places, and perhaps I came to love some of them even more. But by that time I had established a base in Costa Rica. I lived and worked four years in Nicaragua, four years in El Salvador. . . . I've traveled extensively throughout Central America, and there are other peoples that undoubtedly have captured my heart, as peoples. But I always felt that I had made my home in Costa Rica, that this is where I'd come to put down roots.

I was twenty-six when I arrived in this country. And, well, the marriage lasted two and a half years. I now understand—back then I didn't—that my husband was from the upper middle class, maybe the upper class, and he'd been primed by his parents to inherit the family business. His years in the United States were a youthful parenthesis for him, years for getting rebellion out of his system before settling down to the serious business of life. Those were his years to be a revolutionary, to organize the Latin American student community, to be who he might have been. But once we came to Costa Rica, he had to move back into the prescribed mold. Because he was the chosen one, the son who was expected from childhood to take over the family business.

So we got here, and the first thing that happened was that I started working at the University of Costa Rica. I got involved in social action projects. I traveled to rural areas teaching indigenous peoples to read and write—a wonderful experience in which I came in contact with the real culture of this country.

I mean I was a woman accustomed to thinking of food as something that originated in a supermarket, packaged and all, because that's the way I'd seen it in the United States, and in Puerto Rico too. Not in my immediate family, because we fished and ate what we caught. I'm talking about the more general context. About people washing their clothes in washing machines instead of rivers. When I got here I went to work in communities in which the ovens were little caves along the riverbanks, where you determined the heat with a leaf—if the leaf burned then the oven was ready to receive the bread, and if it wasn't quite that hot it was ready for other things. Communities in which we bathed in the river, in which there was no electricity. I was experiencing all this, the real culture of the country, and my husband was moving back into the social groove that would enable him to take over his family's business.

We decided to separate because, obviously, we weren't going to find a common ground in such very different ways of experiencing the world. Besides, at that point, as he prepared to take over the business, what he wanted and needed was a traditional wife who would keep his house and be able to entertain his friends and associates. And he'd already told me that the day I decided to organize politically would be the day our relationship ended. I simply packed my bags. Because from the moment I got here I'd become completely involved with the teachers' union on the campus of the University of Costa Rica.

Those were years of particularly intense struggle, not only in Costa Rica but throughout the entire Central American region. My husband and I separated amicably; we still speak to one another from time to time. And I was here until 1979, when I went to Nicaragua. As soon as the Sandinista revolution came to power. I'd been working in Central America—in El Salvador and Nicaragua—but in 1979 I went to Nicaragua to work in the Sandinista literacy crusade. Literacy has always been my vocation.

María, I have the impression, I've had the impression since we met, that your family has always been very supportive of you, politically supportive, and . . .

Yes, I have what I'd call a very special relationship with my family. Dad and Mom are very special people. I wouldn't call ours a close family exactly, but we stand behind one another in every situation. And my mother and father have always had a very good relationship. Mother is the strong one and Dad's very softhearted; he was the youngest of thirteen brothers and sisters, and more than half of them were girls. So he was the baby in his family. And he turned out to be very sensitive, with his sensitive side super well developed.

Insofar as family negotiations were concerned, this turned out to be very useful. I'm not talking about anything very unusual but a very interesting relationship. My father gave a lot to the family; he worked in order to be able to spend time with us and in order to support us; in that order, not the other way around. He was never the absent father, you know, not physically and not emotionally either.

Mom is a very strong woman, as I say, and she is the one who has broken with the inherited silences—which I've had to work through, of course—silences around the fact that my paternal grandfather was a shoemaker, that sort of thing. Later in life, when my mother started writing, she's had to deal with resistance on both sides of the family. Because she's written about issues they didn't want exposed. The fact that my great-great-grandfather was a shoemaker in the Spanish army, that my other great-great-grandfather owned slaves—all those things she's written about, and it's earned her a number of family conflicts.

One of the most important things I've learned about myself is that my mother didn't want to have girls. And I was the first, the oldest daughter. It was with my birth that my mother had to confront the fact that she did give birth to a girl, and of course I've had to face that as well—with her.

This is a very important issue for me. Because being born a girl, of a mother who didn't want girls, makes for a great deal of ambivalence. On the one hand, it's allowed me a lot of space, but it has been a confusing space. Unacknowledged, not openly talked about, silenced completely. Until I asked my mother to write about her children's births; I think I've already told you about this.

One of the most complicated aspects of my family, one of the most difficult to understand, especially in the relationship with my mother —with my father no, although it might turn out to be the same—is that they have always supported everything I've done, but I felt that their support has somehow been conditional.

And it's interesting, because what haven't I done in my life? I became a nun. In my adolescence I was incredibly rebellious. I mean I tested my parents to extraordinary limits. I was also testing myself of course. And they passed the tests, and so did I. They didn't exactly approve of everything I did, but they never made it impossible for me to do those things.

I went into the convent. Daddy was of the opinion that if that was what I wanted, it was fine; Mommy resisted. I found this out many years later. I didn't even know it at the time. Well, I entered the convent, and then four years later I left the convent. And continuing with the ways in which I tested my parents: the first man I brought home was black, a black man and a gringo to boot, from the United States. Later I married, moved to Costa Rica, and divorced. Then I went off to do literacy work in the guerrilla zones in El Salvador. What I'm saying is that my parents have had to deal with almost every possible challenge, and all of it concentrated in a single one of their children!

Of the six brothers and sisters, are you the only one who's challenged your parents in these ways?

I'm not the only one. The truth is, my parents are also radical in their own way. Only more in line with their generation. But they're plenty radical. My oldest brother is an architect and an artist. And outstanding: he's once of the best potters in the world. He studied architecture, then he quit his profession and became an artist. He's never married, doesn't have children. He's always been a rebel.

Then I have a brother who became a fisherman. He was a tremendous rebel but the sea tamed him, or he let himself be tamed. Whatever his reasons. Today he's married, with stepchildren, and his own fishing business. This brother is brilliant, and very talented; he would have been a marvelous writer. My younger brother is also a rebel in his way. He is a great and very present father to his children.

My other two siblings, the women, lead more ordinary lives. They've got their opinions, they're critical of things, but their lives are the usual—what's expected of women in Puerto Rican society. But they have both been to hell and back and are very strong and determined. The most rebellious among us have been my oldest brother, the brother who's a fisherman, and me. But in Puerto Rico, ours remains an unusual family in the sense that each of us ended up doing what he or she wanted.

Even my two sisters, with their traditional families and all, are happy. They've made the sort of lives they wanted for themselves. And they've demanded respect. They haven't put up with abuse of any kind, not from their husbands or from anyone else. My sisters live ordinary professional and family lives, but not submissive lives or lives of resignation.

What I'm thinking about at this point in my life is what conditional freedom really means. What it means that my parents have always supported my decisions, but with limits. And I haven't been able to completely understand the reasons for those limits, how they are constructed, what they mean.

For one thing, look how I've lived my relationship with my parents. Each of my transgressions, each of my options I've carried out a thousand miles from home. That has to tell you something. It isn't a coincidence that I choose to make my life so far from them. In fact I don't think very many things are coincidental. The first thing this tells you is that you feel—whether or not it's true, that's the part I haven't figured out yet—that you cannot do these things close to home. This in and of itself implies conditionality.

I go home a couple of weeks each year, maybe three. On special occasions. Every Christmas I ask a key question, from among those I've managed to come up with. The last time I was home I asked my mother about her own sexuality. And she said: Do you have three months to listen to my answer? That's as far as she was willing to go. Three years before that I'd asked her what it was like when I was born. I could tell that she wasn't going to be able to answer me, so I asked her to write about our births, all six of them. I wanted to know about my birth, so I asked her about them all.

I keep a lot of secrets with regard to my parents, yet we talk about many other things. And I haven't figured out why. Maybe it's because I haven't come to grips with these issues myself. But through all these years my process has been one of opening a door and walking through it for myself, no limits at all, but rarely sharing it with them. There's got to be a reason. And maybe I'm going to have to find out that their support is not as unconditional as I believed.

For example, I have never discussed my sexual identity with my parents. They haven't wanted to know either. The only people in my family who have wanted to know are my sister, the sister who comes right after me, and my brother. And they do know. They know because they wanted to know. They asked me and I told them. The rest don't want to know.

Of course it's all a bit confusing, too, because I've gone home from time to time with other very close woman friends, women who weren't my partners but with whom I have very close friendships, so who knows? I've introduced my parents to soul mates of mine, women who were in the convent with me, lots of other women. My mother just doesn't want to know. I don't think she wants to deal with it.

And my mother sends me articles, the most incredible articles, they're mostly out of the current backlash [against feminism] but so subtle that she thinks they're feminist. Most recently she sent me one about the vocation for maternity that exists in all women, even in lesbians, even in professional women, etc., etc. She's undoubtedly trying to establish some sort of bridge, maybe even a dialogue, about things that are clearly evident but unspoken between us.

I was telling someone the other day that my mother sends me these articles for a combination of reasons having to do with how she sees me, my involvements, but also having to do with her own life. Painful things in her life that we haven't talked about. For instance, she's a mother who adores all six of her children. She devoted herself to all of us, although she never completely sacrificed her own needs. She didn't sacrifice her professions, though she did stop working for a while when we were young. She's not one of those women who's given everything and not kept anything for herself.

At the same time, she's always had a question about my own vocation for motherhood — or lack of it. She's always wondered. This woman who had six children, who wanted to have seven, wondering about her daughter who didn't have any. In sending me that article I felt that she was trying to reconcile the difference between us. It was an article out of the current backlash, you know, but it was a way of reconciling my life: I didn't have children, but all that I've done has been a kind of social motherhood. It's shit, you know. I have to talk to her about all this. But I understand that this has been my mother's way of reconciling those areas we haven't been able to broach face to face.

It is interesting. But I want to go back to when you decided to enter the convent. I want to understand what induced you to become a nun.

I had a great many questions about society as I was growing up, throughout my adolescence especially. When I was fourteen I was already participating in projects in the slums. And these were projects directed by nuns. My concerns also came from the contrast I saw between my own life and the way people lived in those areas. It was an extreme contrast.

I told you we lived in an upper-class neighborhood, and I attended one of the most elitist schools on the island. At the same time, I spent weeks and months in fishing villages, among fishing people, throughout the country. I was always conscious of the differences, and I always felt that I wanted to use the opportunities I had to help breach the gap between the ways different classes of peoples lived.

I think my mother and father also contributed to giving me that social consciousness, because they never hid those realities from me. On the contrary, they pointed them out, and with some sense of responsibility. It wasn't a matter of other people being poor and we being rich, or of others not having enough to eat when we did. Or that this was just the way things were. No. Daddy would go out to fish one weekend, being a fisherman, and the next he'd be over in the fishing village as an engineer, helping people rebuild their shacks that had been destroyed by the latest tropical storm.

I found an outlet for my social concerns in the work I could do with the nuns, those nuns who were also my teachers. But the other thing that was going on with me then was a certain degree of politicization. The Cuban missile crisis, well the Cuban Revolution as a whole—as I lived it in Puerto Rico, and I'm talking about my early years of junior high school—many of the nuns who were my junior high teachers were exiles from Cuba. They naturally detested the Cuban Revolution. They talked about our great friends the gringos and how the revolution had taken everything from people.

But we students were naturally independentista; we'd grown up with those sentiments, and they formed a part of our developing identities. From my point of view, there's not much difference between the way in which one must break with one's parents and the way in which one's life is affected by colonization: it's a similar process. In Puerto Rico, a kid who didn't consider her or himself an independentista in adolescence wasn't going to develop a mature identity.

So for me, it wasn't really the faith component of religion that drew me, although religion certainly had a faith component to it for me then. My parents were both religious, my mother less than my father. But as I emerged from adolescence, I saw in the convent the possibility of a life devoted to social change, and a life that wouldn't be wasted on the frivolities that bored me: those superficial dances, the endless social activities at the club, all that sort of thing. As an adolescent I felt satiated with that life.

So I decided I wanted to become a religious sister, and I chose the order of the nuns of my childhood. I saw them as the most liberal. They were the Dominican Sisters of Newburgh, New York. I saw them as the most liberal because they were free thinkers and so forth. If I had known about liberation theology at the time, I might have skipped the convent and ended up in a Christian base community.

I was looking for a community. But—and this is something I came to understand much later—not just a women's community. I was looking for a structure that was authoritarian and liberal at one and the same time. I've often told my friends this, and they've thought me crazy. For me, the convent was the perfect transition for a woman who came out of a very secure family structure, a very stable home situation, and who had to go out into the world as an independent person, completely on her own. Because my mother was very clear on that point—she raised us all to be independent. The convent was the perfect transition for me: a women's community, liberal but with its authoritarian structure.

I was able to leave my family of origin without taking it with me. The whole first year, for example, I was only allowed a single phone call home. I could write letters, but I couldn't see my family, and they couldn't tell me what to do.

Back then I saw the convent as the perfect context in which to develop myself. When I talk about authority, what I mean is that there was an imposition of very clear limits. But limits for me have always been meant to be transgressed. And I transgressed them all.

Which was something I didn't really have at home. Because, as I've said, Mom and Dad supported me in everything I wanted to do, but I was somehow never really clear about where the limits were. There were always things that remained unspoken, those famous silences.

In the convent, on the other hand, everything was absolutely clear: the rules, the traditions, what one could and couldn't do. And it wasn't my family, so I was able to transgress, experiment with my transgressions without having to risk the parental relationship. My parents weren't even going to know what I did or didn't do.

I was also pretty clear that marriage wasn't my primary goal. What better community, then, for a woman who wanted to be socially useful and study at the same time? I'd always wanted to be a teacher, from as far back as I can remember. Mommy tells me I talked about being a teacher from the time I was three. I never wanted to be anything else. The Dominican Sisters were a teaching order, so entering the convent allowed me to study to become a teacher and to work for social change.

Much much later—when I found the women's community, when I discovered feminism—I understood that the convent, for me, was also a safe place, a place where I could learn to transgress and do what I wanted to do, protected by the safety of an all-women's space. It was a women's community. Later I understood this but not when I entered.

And I've come to the conclusion, talking with friends—some of whom have been nuns and some not—that the convent is an excellent transition in this respect. Because it's a transition within a women's world, within a well-defined structure but one in which staying or not staying is voluntary. As well as what you do or don't do.

In the convent, the limits aren't yours alone. You see them reflected as well in a group of different women. There were eighteen of us. And I'd say all of us were more or less atheists. Secular in nature, so to speak. We were all pretty rebellious: a class of novitiates very much within the tradition of Vatican II.[1]

Our class entered in 1966. The documents from Vatican II, from the early sixties, those were revolutionary documents. And those were the premises upon which we entered. That was what we intended to do with our lives, that was what we wanted. Of the eighteen, we were three Latin Americans and fifteen from different parts of the United States, most of them from New York, the eastern part of the country. Almost all of us came from schools run by the same congregation, most of them located in New York, New Jersey, around there. A few of the women were from the South.

We built a beautiful community, among ourselves and with the older sisters too. For a young woman, coming directly out of high school, there aren't that many opportunities to study in a community of women from different generations. There wasn't that much cultural diversity, and even less racial difference. Most of us were young white women, which is the nature of Catholicism in the United States.

The truth is, it was a fabulous experience. The community we were able to create, the spiritual bonds we developed, how well we got to know one another, and the opportunity for study. Because I'd been a really poor student in high school. I didn't even know I was intelligent. And what intelligence I did know I had, I used just to get by. That's how Mommy always says I developed my intelligence back then, figuring out exactly what I needed to do in order to just make it. Structured learning didn't really interest me that much then. Which is why I didn't think of myself as intelligent.

I wanted to be a teacher, and so I was passionately interested in college, and by that time I was interested in what I was studying. I was finally getting good grades. But I also had the perfect context in which to study, without the pressure of dating, of boys, of all those other activities. And in a community that supported what I wanted to do.

We did our academic work at a local university, Newburgh College, which belonged to the nuns, a very good professional school. We studied there along with the other lay students. The professors were Dominican sisters.

Of course I wondered about the other seventeen women in that group of novitiates. Was María still in contact with any of them? Had they remained in the convent, had some of them left, and if so where were they now?

Recently I've tried to reestablish contact. And five years ago I went back to visit the convent, which was very interesting. But lately I've tried to reestablish contact; we'd continued to be in touch with one another, and then we drifted apart after a while. All eighteen of us left the convent, all eighteen of us. Not a single woman in my group stayed!

And we helped one another leave. Even while some were still in the convent, they visited those of us who had left. We even helped one of our group who was from India, a cloistered student they'd brought over to study because she was so brilliant. Imagine, a cloistered nun, in India, in Bombay, who'd been in a convent from the time she was thirteen! She was so brilliant she earned a scholarship from Fordham University to come over and study physics. Her order allowed her to dispense with the cloistered life in order to study in the United States. But of course she had to continue to live in a convent, and so she lived in ours.

When she arrived, that young woman didn't speak a single word of English. And we decided that we were going to be her mothers. We went through the whole process with her, teaching her to drop the habit and start wearing regular clothes. (We were still using the habit when I entered; I'll show you the pictures.) We said it would be better for her if she attended Fordham dressed in ordinary clothing, but we also learned from her how the habit can protect a woman. At first she was frightened to go to class without her habit. The habit not only identified her as a nun but it also isolated her from others. And she wanted to be isolated from certain people. I learned about all that from her.

But this woman did drop the habit and begin to wear civilian clothes. And she fell in love. She fell in love with a young man who was also from India and was studying at the same school. And then we taught her—and we also learned along with her—how she could remain in the convent so as not to lose her scholarship or the possibility of living free of cost.

At the same time, we talked about the fact that she mustn't feel obliged to marry this man, just to have a place to live. We taught her how to live the world's most marvelous hypocrisy. We advised her to marry the man she loved but to continue living in the convent as if she were single—until she could finish her studies. I lost contact with this woman, but someday I'll find her again.

There were five of us who were involved with helping this woman from India; we designed the perfect strategy for her . . . the whole thing was an extraordinary experience. Once she graduated, she even had to ask for special dispensation from the pope in order to get married. It was all planned, down to the last detail. I think I first became a strategist in that situation, and a strategist in clandestine conditions:

the perfectly measured steps that needed to be taken and when, all the discussions about what was ethical and why. How it could be ethically correct even when it didn't appear to be, although it seemed like hypocrisy. It was a marvelous experience!

So it was all that, understand? The group of us were also the great transgressors in the convent, in the sense that we measured everything we did in order to be able to act not in accordance with the Church but in line with what we knew was right. We had our own humanitarian goals. For example, when we were caught doing something completely out of line — out of line was, for instance, when we had to wash our white habits. We had industrial-sized washing machines, the size of this room, and we'd purposely put those white habits in there to wash along with two red towels!

On Sunday, every one of the two hundred nuns appeared in pink habits! So they punished us. And the punishment was that from then on we had to serve breakfast to the elderly nuns and attend to their needs. Many of them were over a hundred years old. They were all up on the seventh floor. And we knew that the priest would take his time eating his breakfast, and then around nine o'clock he'd go up to the seventh floor to give holy communion to those ancient nuns who could no longer come to chapel.

We didn't feel this was right, for those elderly women, many of whom were senile, to have to wait for their breakfast until after the priest had his. They were nuns of the old guard, who weren't going to eat until they'd taken communion. So we decided to get up early and pretend we were the priest; we'd give those nuns an unsanctified host, they thought they'd taken communion, they had their breakfast at seven and didn't have to go hungry. When the priest arrived, for all they knew it was the next morning!

That was the kind of thing we delighted in; the host was never that holy to us! Our strategies were always interesting. And all of this created in us in a very particular identity, a very particular rebellion. We transformed our punishments into social action. When you are able to take rules and regulations you don't believe are just and transform them into something that makes sense to you, has meaning within your system of values, that's when you're able to create alternative ways of life. I don't know if eventually they would have thrown me out. Because I quit before they could.

Remember when they killed those students at Kent State? Well, we studied alongside lay students at the university. It was the era of Vatican II, social justice issues were on the agenda, and when we heard about what had been perpetrated at Kent State, five of us decided—we didn't think twice—that the most logical thing for us to do was to demonstrate, like so many were doing at other universities all across the United States.

As nuns, we were the link—within a super-conservative community like Newburgh—between the Puerto Rican ghetto in which I worked at the Head Start program, the black neighborhood, and the middle-class white university students. We lived and/or worked in all three communities. And so of course we organized a march, and the three sectors took part. We all marched together, and the other students asked us—in our habits—to march out in front. They thought maybe if the police saw nuns they wouldn't use their tear gas. By then we knew how to make good use of our habits!

What disappointed me about the reaction to that march, on the part of the convent, well, when the Mother Superior called us in, it wasn't so much that we'd taken part in a protest against the murder of the students at Kent State—although she certainly didn't approve of that—what really bothered her was the fact that blacks, Puerto Ricans, and whites had marched together! I was indignant. Right then and there I said I can't stay here any longer. It would have been bad enough if they'd have told us that as nuns we shouldn't have demonstrated publicly. I wouldn't have stood for that either. But to oppose the coming together of the three communities that fed my personal identity: that was something I wasn't going to take. It was racism pure and simple.

By the time they called us in, we already had our bags packed. Ciao. Ciao. That's another important issue. It's important to try to define how we women process that moment, when do we say they kicked me out and when do we say I left. It's extraordinarily important, especially as women, that we understand what we do as opposed to what is done to us, and that we claim that, in order to understand the nature of power.

It's also true that this can change at different moments in our lives. You yourself said, just a while back, that you entered the convent for a series of reasons. Among them, that you'd never wanted to get married. And then, later, you got married.

It's not that I'd never thought about getting married. It's just that it wasn't my main goal, as it was for so many other young women of my generation. And it also had to do with what I saw as my mandate. Mandate and transgression: it's this conflict that interests me so much.

My mother, for example, didn't marry until she finished her studies. She was my father's girlfriend from the time she was thirteen. But she decided she wasn't going to get married until she had her degree. And she married at twenty-six, the same as I did.

Let's talk more about mandates and transgressions.

One of the most difficult things for us women is learning to distinguish between the mandates and the transgressions. What we may think are mandates may really be transgressions, and what we think are transgressions may be mandates. And we have trouble distinguishing precisely because what we hear as the voices of mandate are the ones we think come from inside. And what we hear as the voices of transgression are the ones we think come only from outside. That's why we have so much trouble recognizing rage, recognizing how dissatisfied we are, the whole way we've been socialized.

The problem of mandates and transgressions is very complex because it crosses subjective lines as well as coming down through our main authority figures: the mother, the father if there is one, even siblings, whether they be older or younger than we are, and through our female condition itself. In my case it was important that my mother didn't want girls and that I was her firstborn girl. I always say this gave me the great privilege of dual socialization.

The fact that one is simultaneously undesired as a girl and yet socialized to be a little girl: that's a tremendous contradiction. A girl who is desired, and socialized to be a little girl, or a man who is born into a world that expects certain things of men: these conditions too spawn contradictions. Because we all have much more to give than the gendered roles society expects of us.

For example, I remember throughout my childhood, and particularly when I had my first period—that was a tremendous crisis for me. I was raised with very ambivalent mandates. They provided me with a great deal of space. At the same time, they probably prevented me from having . . . well, I don't know whether to call it security . . . yes, they did keep me from developing a certain sense of security. When you adopt certain roles and comply with their mandates, you develop a sense of security that you don't get when you transgress. I'm thinking about the fact that I bit my fingernails until about fifteen years ago. I wet my bed until I was ten. At forty-eight, I'm still smoking like a chimney, and I haven't been able to stop.[2] Anxiety is a product of ambivalence, but it's also a product of liking that ambivalence. I had to learn to understand mine.

When I became a feminist and realized that I didn't fit into any of the categories of gender socialization, that was when I had to ask myself the question. It wasn't just that I didn't fit. All the boys' games: I was taught to be active, aggressive, you know. My mother wanted a boy and got a girl. There were never any limits on my play. And I never felt, at home, that the boys did certain things and the girls others.

Until I got to school. But even there . . . I had to deal with something else, which was that I am left-handed. And my mother, who you will remember was a teacher, prepared me well for the outside world. She told me I must never permit an assault upon my condition as a left-handed person. Don't you ever let them try to make you write with your right hand, she said.

But what happened to me at school was that, although they didn't try to make me write with my right hand, they tried to make me position my notebook like a right-handed person. And I wouldn't let them. When the teacher came over and tried to turn my notebook around, I resisted. As that teacher attempted to change my writing habits, the other students started murmuring and such. The teacher got angry and tapped her ruler against my desk. But she missed the desk and hit me on the hand instead.

I didn't think twice. I hit her back. My mother was called to the school, of course. And she defended me. What's more, she reasoned with me: that I shouldn't be hitting my teacher but that I didn't have to let her hit me either. Much less did I have to put up with her trying to turn my notebook around.

That was my mother's great virtue. When we've talked about it, it seems to me that she worried that I might have been irritated by that ambivalence; the truth is, it's been a blessing. Whatever the social construction of ambivalence, it's always also a curse—but in that sense we're all cursed, every one of us. Because gender construction itself is a limiting condition. It limits men as well as women, but it limits women so much more.

I think it's actually more complex. There are a whole series of issues here that we don't yet understand. Because another young girl growing up as you did might have experienced what you interpreted as ambivalence as an intolerable set of mixed messages. What provides freedom for one may cause extreme discomfort and uncertainty in another. Why do you think, María, that in your case your mother's ambivalence ultimately gave you space?

You're right. Of course there are other factors involved. In my case I believe one of the most important elements in my formation is that—as far as I can tell—I was never a victim of abuse. Well, ambivalence itself is abusive. But it's not intentionally abusive. It's simply a reflection of the institutionalized violence implicit in gender construction. My mother lived this and passed it on to me. But as far as I know I never experienced incest; there was no physical or psychological or even verbal abuse in my childhood home. And I grew up thinking that all the little girls and boys in the world were as happy as I was.

I grew up in a cruel world, but I grew up protected, supported, with a sense of security that we now know is unusual. The ambivalence was there, it's true, but I think these other factors also made a difference. I've spoken to so many women who were abused as children—either sexually or through some other abuse of power—and they've told me how they used to get down on their knees and plead with God to turn them into men.

I know a great many women who grew up wanting to be male. In my case, where there was sexual abuse—I was incested by my maternal grand- parents—there was also the buffer created by my parents, who respected and at least tried to protect me. This is another element that sometimes functions to preserve a measure of self-esteem: where there's protection, of whatever kind, growth is possible.

That's right. For me, the issue of defying limits—the mandates and the transgressions—has been very important. That's why I've talked so much about this. It's been important to me in thinking about my life. I grew up feeling that my mandates included being a woman, a woman of the middle classes, and also an ambivalent woman. And then there was the fact that I was Puerto Rican. Those were the voices I had going for me, and which I had to assimilate, internalize somehow. For in- stance, as a middle-class woman, I never doubted that I would get a good education, have a profession. I always say that I chose to be a teacher. But my family was full of teachers. My mother was a teacher.

I thought I was making a choice. But there you have an example of a mandate without transgression. Because of course teaching is a ser- vice profession. It's true, I've been extraordinarily happy as a teacher. Another mandate for me was to be intelligent. No question about that. Because for a woman to become a professional, and for a middle-class woman to be able to compete in the professional world, she had to be intelligent.

I was also supposed to want to marry. From the time you are a little girl, people ask you if you have a boyfriend yet, who you have a crush on, the whole nine yards. And in my case, the boys were my buddies; we played baseball and volleyball together. But then what I was told was: well, don't forget to let them win once in a while. In my family I was encouraged to play with the boys, and to play with them on a more or less equal footing. But once in a while, let them win!

If that wasn't ambivalence, I don't know what was. Still, they never prevented me from playing with boys. Many of the games I played were boys' games, although I loved playing dolls, and girls' games were also a part of my world.

Marriage was another of my mandates. And another was a natural byproduct of my being born Puerto Rican: the expected attitude of rebellion when faced with the power of the United States. In this case, rebellion was okay. But it was also complicated, because the school my parents sent me to was run by U.S. sisters. In that sense, the expected response wasn't a frontal rebellion but simply part of our identity construct.

From early on, these are the mandates that were important in my life. And I transgressed them all, or almost all.

I think entering a convent, for many women in recent years, has been complex. I have so many friends, women like you, from the United States and elsewhere, who entered a religious order at a particular moment in their development. Many of them stayed a few years, long enough to mature and acquire a profession, long enough to become involved in the social service community, and then they left, as you did.

I think it would be interesting to read a study of this phenomenon, if one exists. I wonder how many of these women simply needed a community of women, didn't want to be forced into marrying a man, felt the need of a space in which they might grow—a women's space, a safe space, a supportive space in which they could do social or political work.

Don't forget the negation of the body. That figures into some young women's early desire to be nuns. But in my case there was a sort of reverse phenomenon there. My first period produced a crisis. I'm still trying to understand the full dimension of how that affected me.

When you're an athlete like I was, you discover other bodies early on. You're constantly looking at other bodies, almost nude. And I was a swimmer. So you develop a consciousness about your own body's potential, about controlling your body—at least insofar as physical exercise is concerned. You develop that consciousness, push it to its limits.

I have a great many friends who tell me they weren't really conscious of their bodies until they started menstruating. A great many women. Because I was an athlete it was different. I had a great consciousness of my own body until I had my first period.

It's interesting. Because in a certain sense that's the very opposite of how we're socialized. When we begin menstruating, when we become women, as they say, that's when most of us really begin to see our bodies in their most conditioned roles: to be used for this or that, to serve this or that purpose. None of which may be natural to a particular woman's character or physical makeup.

That's right. And I've wanted to understand how that happened for me because, as I say, I've listened to a lot of my friends—middle-class North Americans, middle-class Africans, from the Philippines, from all sorts of places—who have told me that they had a sense of their own bodies as children, but that as they grew up, being from the middle classes and with the mandate of becoming professionals, they came to think of themselves almost as intellects with legs.

I got the opposite message. I was involved in sports; I was a swimmer. And growing up I wasn't that interested in developing my intellect. I wasn't interested in studying, mainly because I detested the awful educational system that was imposed upon us. So it's been interesting to me, talking to these friends, because it's always revealing to be able to find oneself reflected in difference, not just commonality.

As far as marriage was concerned, I saw it both as mandate and as something to be resisted. Many times over [she laughs]. There was also a great deal of ambivalence. For example, I think my first marriage was some sort of test or exercise. I needed to discover for myself that marriage wasn't for me.

I have tremendous admiration for my mother and father, and for the relationship they've been able to build—between the two of them, with all of us, and also with the community as a whole. Still, from the time I was very young, I understood that Mommy had a great deal more potential than what she was able to express in her marriage. Her marriage put too much weight on her shoulders.

I thought to myself, if I want to be a teacher, why would I want to have six children and a husband to take care of? Always dealing with the social image and so forth. So I ended up trying marriage with a number of different men, in a number of different ways. And I moved beyond them all. You won't find me marrying again, not a man in any case!

But those marriages left me a lot besides pain. They taught me that if I ever really gave myself to marriage, the way a marriage should be, I was going to have to give up a lot of what I wanted to do for myself. And for others.

The other mandate and transgression about which I want to speak concerns motherhood. Here too I tried including it in my life, and I ended up rejecting it. I'm not a mother, not in the biological sense. I've had one miscarriage—with my first husband, back when I wanted to have children. And I don't really believe that losing a child is coincidental. I lived those two months of pregnancy with a lot of ambivalence. I had a miscarriage when I thought I wanted to have a child.

I've adopted scores of children—in El Salvador and elsewhere—and I also have many friends who have made me their children's adoptive mother, or I have made myself their adoptive mother.

Maternity, for me, has been a mixture of mandate and transgression. And my final decision in that arena was when I realized I didn't want to experience biological motherhood. I made that one when I was thirty-eight years old—ten years ago now—when I had to leave the liberated zone in El Salvador and go to Guatemala. A doctor there told me I had cysts on my uterus. He said I could leave them alone if I wanted to, but I'd have to have a checkup every three months. Imagine, in the mountains of El Salvador you don't get to see a doctor in years, let alone every three months!

I finally decided to have a hysterectomy. That's when I reconciled my relationship to motherhood once and for all. That's when I finally dealt with my ambivalence about having or not having children. And I was able to deal with it because I no longer felt guilty. I haven't always been able to speak publicly about having had an abortion—because abortion is still illegal here. But among friends I've been able to discuss the fact that I've experienced both sides of the question.

People say it's not the same to lose a child you want and one that isn't wanted. I know the difference. When I was pregnant, during my first marriage, and I wanted the child—whether because I'd been taught to want it or because I really did—I felt the loss as if it were a part of myself. For six months following that miscarriage, I'd wake up in the middle of the night crying bitterly: my period had come.

Imagine, speaking of body response, I've never been one to experience problems with menstruation, but for six months after that miscarriage I'd know when I was going to start my period because I'd wake up crying in the night. But years later, when I had an abortion because that was what I decided I wanted, I didn't experience any of that. I felt that second pregnancy as something outside myself, something not desired. So I've lived both those experiences. And I reconciled myself to not being a mother—a physiological mother—when they took a part of my reproductive system from me. My uterus.

Well, what other mandates are there? There's the mandate around the issue of power. We women are raised to see power as something outside or beyond ourselves: power is dirty, it's bad. And then feminism comes along and reiterates that power is patriarchal, so it remains bad, dirty, and all that. What do we do with this?

In my case, because of my particular characteristics, what my mother expected of me, how she raised me to be independent, autonomous, to have self-esteem . . . certainly there was ambivalence there, but with these characteristics clearly predetermined. I think I always had a measure of power. And I was aware of that.

In my case the message was: sure, you can achieve power, but not in relation to men. Because they won't like it, no one will want to marry you, all those ideas. Always let the boys win. Don't be so assertive, don't fight with them. I remember my first boyfriend. My first boyfriend was a neighbor of ours; he lived two houses down the street. I must have been eight or ten years old.

We played tennis, that little boy and I. And I remember inviting him out to play a game of tennis. I asked him! That was considered a date, my first date. And when I went to pick him up, all dressed in my tennis whites with my racket in my hand—and remember, I'd asked him: that in itself was a transgression—he stuck his head out the window and called down that he didn't want to go. Well, I picked up three good-sized stones and threw them at that window.

Now there was a transgression for you! And he was just a little friend, not really a boyfriend at that age. I wasn't sorry for what I'd done, although it cost me. It cost me my friend, it cost me one hell of a verbal beating—and I hadn't even broken the window because it was made of aluminum. But Margaret, I really believe in our first responses to those events that are critical in our lives, the events that mark us. That was my first date, so to speak. The boy told me he didn't want to go, and I turned around and hurled three rocks at him.

But of course this was preadolescence. Later, in adolescence, things got murkier. There was more ambivalence. Because by then there was the added element of one's friends, the social pressures, fear of getting pregnant—all those things. Then I lived the power equation much more uneasily. I might simply turn away or leave, if I felt threatened. But I wasn't going to give up my self-determination, my power. I think this also had a lot to do with my mother. The only thing a guy ever had to do was insinuate that I couldn't do what I wanted. That was enough. All I had to do was smell injustice, of any kind, and I was out of there.

On the other hand, I haven't always felt comfortable with power. I've often felt guilt, considerable guilt. And there have been times when although I haven't exactly offered up my own power, I have submitted myself to authoritarian structures. This was true with some of the organizations on the Left, and certainly when I was in the convent.

It wasn't a matter of my doing everything I was ordered to do. If it didn't seem right to me, I'd get out of it somehow. But you know the contradiction here, what I haven't been able to figure out to this day? I always looked for markedly authoritarian structures, so I could break with those structures from the inside. Maybe I needed to have those clear limits in order to transgress them without ambivalence. As I think about it now, I understand it a lot better.

It wasn't until I found feminism, or maybe even a bit later, that I began to accept and understand that I myself needed to replace my structures, time and time again. Or that I don't need to place myself in such patriarchal structures to begin with. Rather than always breaking down or breaking out, now I am able to create my own structures, to affirm instead of destroy. And it was then that I founded FIRE, and the women's human rights project in CODEHUCA, the Commission for the Defense of Human Rights in Central America. I didn't have to keep working inside the traditional structures, where one always has to struggle. I could create my own.

And I think it's been the same in my personal life with regard to power relationships. You spend such a long time struggling, fighting against the different unjust power structures. And the time comes when you simply want to create. Of course the ambivalence continues to be there. Besides the guilt we tend to feel, there's that old ambivalence: resistance and affirmation. But not necessarily linear. You can't fight all the battles, at least not all of them at once. This was also important for me to understand.

Speaking of mandates and transgressions, I'm also very interested in another area in which these play an important part. Of course I'm interested in the whole revolutionary piece: how you opted to work in certain organizations, do a particular kind of revolutionary work. But I'm also interested in the professional side of all that: your choice to leave the university, to leave the stability of your profession and strike out to work in areas that don't include that sort of stability, that have no health insurance or pension plan or benefit package, not even a future in many cases.

First, let's talk about the revolutionary options. I'm not as interested in naming the organizations or knowing the details of the work as I am in

the process that led you to make the choices. The revolutionary organiza-
tions of the seventies, especially, were men's domains.

Okay, remember, I always fit very well into men's domains. And I could just as easily have fit into women's domains. I'd been prepared for both. My political life really began in the United States, in the struggle for bilingual education—which also crossed over into my professional life. Maybe my political life began in earnest when I came to Costa Rica, when I got involved in struggles through the university.

I'm talking about 1974. It was a time of great upheaval here, and throughout Central America things were very critical, very difficult. Here in Costa Rica I became involved in the struggle for neighborhood rights. I identified with the people in the communities out of the experience I'd had in the United States and out of my early Christian experience. In other words, I identified with social struggle out of my Latin American identity, which was accentuated by my identity as a Puerto Rican.

As a Puerto Rican, the anti-imperialist nature of all these struggles was very familiar to me. But the Costa Ricans were waging their own struggles, and they were Costa Rican in nature or, in a larger sense, Central American. I worked in peasant communities. I taught literacy, and I organized and trained literacy instructors from the university. I also worked with people in the factories, men and women. But there was no gender component to my consciousness at that time, much less a feminist consciousness of any kind. It was class struggle, pure and simple, what we called revolutionary struggle back then.

This was the identification that linked me to the Sandinistas, to the Farabundistas,[3] to the Guatemalan guerrilla movement. . . . Costa Rica provided tremendous solidarity to all those struggles. There was a rearguard structure here that worked to support each of them, and there were great numbers of refugees. And of course I worked with the refugees as well, organizing literacy campaigns and such.

The Costa Rican Left entered into crisis in 1979, because a great many of us were doing solidarity work with peoples of other countries, and our local situation got lost in the shuffle. The Left here entered into a profound identity crisis then, and I resolved that crisis for myself by simply continuing to work with whomever. I felt equally identified with them all.

In 1979 I went to Nicaragua to take part in the Sandinista's literacy crusade. And you know, Margaret, I've always tried to link my revolutionary work with my profession, because I'm absolutely passionate about my profession and always have been. I've always believed that my profession was essential to social change in that it encourages people's participation. It means democratization, not only a democratization of knowledge but of people's participation as well. That's what popular education is all about.

Right there is an issue that's been very important in the United States, and perhaps elsewhere as well. You chose a profession that is so extraordinarily socially useful, more than useful really: it's work that changes society, really contributes to social change. And you became a revolutionary through that door.

In the United States, at least for many of my generation, our experience was exactly the opposite. At least in the beginning. Too many of us joined political organizations and said: here I am, ready and willing, take me and do with me what you will. Almost religious in essence. Particularly the women. We were willing—for a time at least—to serve the coffee, type the manifestos, follow the orders. We wanted to make the revolution, and our professional lives had to wait. Of course later we rebelled against all that, demanded full integration, and when we didn't get it, started our own organizations. . . .

For me it was always a point of contention—I mean I resisted the orders of many of my superiors because I was never willing to give up my profession. And when I gave it up, it was because I wanted to give it up. I was never willing to become a party professional. Nor was I willing to give up everything. Although I did give everything up on many occasions. Anyway, I went off to the literacy crusade in Nicaragua, in 1979, and I was doing what I loved best: being a teacher.

I learned a great deal with the Sandinistas. The year 1979 was the honeymoon year for the Nicaraguan people, and for me. I considered it a great privilege. Not that I thought I didn't deserve that privilege. But it was a privilege: being able to take part in the great hope of people's participation, the creativity, the idea that the revolution had been won in order to satisfy a people's real needs. Needs people had had for generations, which had never been satisfied. That was a marvelous year and a half.

Afterward I returned to Costa Rica. Because I had yet to resolve my situation at the university. I had asked for time off without pay, and I hadn't decided what to do about that. I hadn't formally left the university. So I came back for one semester, intending to return to Nicaragua—or wherever.

When I returned to the University of Costa Rica, the Salvadoran refugees—through their teachers organization, which was ANDES June 21st—asked if I would be willing to organize a regional literacy campaign in Central America, for the Salvadoran refugees who were by then scattered in camps throughout the region.

I thought: what a wonderful opportunity. I would be able to take what I'd learned in Nicaragua and extend it throughout the region. So I went to work, and I was able to legitimate it all through a social action project at the University of Costa Rica. That's how I came to travel to the different countries, preparing literacy teachers in the refugee camps. And that's how I happened to be in Honduras in 1982, when the events that sparked this interview took place.

There were Salvadoran refugees in Nicaragua, in Honduras, in all the Central American countries, with the exception of Guatemala—because in Guatemala they simply killed them off. Those were wonderful years for me, marvelous years, in which I was able to train so many young men and women, to teach reading and writing with a revolutionary spirit. And my work during those years also put me in very close touch with the areas of El Salvador that were controlled by the guerrillas.

There were so many refugees who spent a week or so in one of the camps and the next week in one of the liberated zones. And those people made me see that there were a great many people in the liberated zones—as they called them in El Salvador at the time—people just like them but who had no one to train them. I was training popular educators to develop their own literacy programs. It wasn't that I myself was teaching people to read and write; I was teaching the people to teach their own, training popular educators.

And they would beg me: if you'd just go for a short time, if you'd just go long enough to set up the programs, set up the schools, it would be a wonderful thing for all of us. I was undecided for a while, but finally I decided to go. And the results of making that choice have been incalculable. I wouldn't have had half that experience had I stayed on at the university.

For me it was a privilege to be able to go to the front lines in El Salvador, to teach reading and writing there, because among other things I was going to be able to live in the present something of what the future promised. And that possibility fascinated me. Who gets the chance to pass from the present to the future just like that? But I lived four years in those liberated zones, and it was hard. I learned that there was really nothing there for us women.

I left the liberated zones of El Salvador, I went to Nicaragua to have a hysterectomy, and I found even more evidence of what I'd been through as a woman. I found women comrades—wives of commanders, some of them commanders themselves—whose husbands had left them for younger women. All the usual shit. And the Party had told them to write about their experiences so they would understand what had happened. What could they write? They were depressed, paralyzed, demoralized.

These women asked me, after my hysterectomy, after three weeks of pondering all this myself, and without having had any formal contact with feminism at that point, from a purely personal, empirical, point of view, they asked me to write for them. I told them no, I couldn't write for them. I might be able to write my own book, out of my own experience, and include the anecdotes many of them had shared with me. I said I'd write the book and we could all discuss it.

I wrote because of what I've heard you say, Margaret, about the reasons for many of your own books: that you find yourself exploring certain problems through the process of writing about them. I had to make sense of my own experience, what I'd lived through, including the hysterectomy, and including the fact that this future we women were supposed to be living in the present had been truncated for us. We were wearing ourselves out in the present for a future that might not come to be.

That book was also important later, because it allowed me to approach the feminist option out of my own life experience. I came back here to San José. I was still convalescing from the hysterectomy, and I was also waiting for my orders, for the contacts that would make it possible for me to return to the front in El Salvador.

It was in the writing of that book that I explored my own gender consciousness. The process was a mixture of self-preservation and learning how to share responsibility for what was going on. But I also gave the book to the comrades in the different organizational structures to read—the men as well as the women. I had some fifteen photocopies made. I gave the first ones to the women who were in Nicaragua with me, and to the male comrade who was my immediate superior. I didn't use names, not even war names, only initials, to protect those involved, and to protect myself. But everyone knew who was who. My descriptions were pretty transparent.

For example, I had written about the fact that I'd had to struggle for three years simply to be allowed to go to the front. Not only to do literacy work. I was involved in the organizational structure itself. And still, I couldn't get the permission. And then the moment I became involved in a relationship with one of the FMLN leaders in Nicaragua, and his wife found out, in no time at all I was sent to the front. My request suddenly became the ideal justification for getting me out of the way. I managed to achieve in a week what I hadn't been able to achieve in three years of legitimate struggle. If I'd known that was the way to do it, I wouldn't have waited so long!

Even though I only used initials, the identities were pretty obvious, and everyone who read the book knew who was who. Which became subversive of course. There was a veritable witch-hunt around that book of mine; they took it from the women's dresser drawers, from under their pillows; they gathered up the copies and prohibited its circulation.

On the other hand Manlio Argueta, who is a Salvadoran writer of note, read the book and was fascinated. He said: This book has to be published; we have to get permission to publish it. He actually spoke with the commander in chief, with Chus, who was at the front. Just recently, three months ago, I saw Manlio again, and he told me that he did obtain permission back then. But Chus died. He was killed in battle.

The FMLN commander who was in Nicaragua at the time, and who had been my partner, decided to ignore Chus's orders, and he continued confiscating copies of the manuscript. Of course the book had exposed him. And so I was back in Costa Rica, waiting for my orders, when I received word from Nicaragua that I wouldn't be going back to El Salvador. They said things were very difficult and so forth, that I should stay on in Nicaragua and work from there.

I responded to that revolutionary order by arguing that what they were doing was punishing me, that there was no real reason to take this line with me, and what I continued to want was to return to the front. If I had to obey that order, I said, well I was out of there. And that's what happened. I left Nicaragua and came back to Costa Rica.

And that's when I went to work for CODEHUCA. That's where I began to push the area of *los derechos de las humanas* (women's human rights), and that's also where I first came in contact with a number of feminists, many of them old friends of mine from the Left, Costa Rican women as well as women from other countries in the region.

I begin to deepen my feminist consciousness considerably, always in collaboration with the Left and with human rights as the issue around which to center my struggle. The women's human rights project provoked a tremendous backlash for me within the human rights commission. A terrible backlash: they accused me of being a lesbian, of being a traitor, any epithet you can think of. They said I'd forsaken my revolutionary values and that the women's human rights project was diversionary in nature, created to take attention away from the revolution itself.

By that time we had a really terrific group of educators working together, and I was sick of being chastised, punished, attacked. My eyes were open. I was also tired of always having to assume a defensive attitude. I was done with all that. From then on, I wanted my battles to be affirmative, to build rather than constantly having to fight for space.

And it was at this point—the goddess must have been hard at work!—that I got a call from Genevieve Vaughan and other feminist women interested in putting together a project of shortwave radio. Within fifteen days I was heading the project, after having made sure I was leaving the work at CODEHUCA in good hands. And the women's human rights project continues to this day with a very solid organizational base.

I went on to coordinate FIRE. I was eager to begin working in a truly feminist collective, one in which we ourselves created and ran things. It's been at FIRE that I've learned how to negotiate, and a whole series of other skills.

I want you to talk a lot more about FIRE, the work you've done there, the reach of the project, the sort of programming you offer. But there's something I want to be sure we touch on before we leave this previous era of your life behind.

From my original interview with you and Nora in Managua, I have the details of 1982: the kidnapping, the days spent in that series of clandestine prisons, the torture, and your eventual release. What I don't have is your return to Costa Rica, following those events. How did you emerge from them? What was it like for you to come back here? How did you deal with what you'd been through? I'm thinking that what you endured had to mark you in all sorts of ways: politically, emotionally, physically, psychologically.

I don't know if you've been able to process any of this. What it meant to survive. How it changed you. What I'd like you to try to do now is to go

back—insofar as that's possible—and situate yourself in that time: the
hours, the days, the weeks following your release and your return to Costa
Rica. What was it like? What changed for you in a practical, everyday
sense? What was taken away from you, and what, if anything, had you
gained?

When I boarded that plane in Honduras, I was the happiest woman in
the world. All I wanted was to get out of that country. You know I was
followed until I actually boarded the plane. And although of course I
knew about what was going on in our countries—the disappearances,
the torture—it is one thing is to know about it and another thing to
live it. I'd say this was the main thing that changed for me: I lost my
innocence.

Although only partially, and I'll tell you why. Life and death form a
duality for me. I boarded that plane dirty, smelling like shit, wearing
the same clothes I'd had on for the past ten days—well, Nora recently
reminded me that we did change our pants, that we took some pants
from the warehouse of clothing designated for the refugees, but there
wasn't really all that much opportunity to get cleaned up.

All I wanted was to get back to Costa Rica. And I didn't want to have
to talk to anyone, or for anyone to try to talk to me. I took my seat on
that plane, and even though I don't drink, I told the flight attendant:
bring me a double shot of whiskey. The plane hadn't even lifted off.
Not all the passengers were even in their seats. The flight attendant
looked at me and said: once we're in the air . . . but I cut her off. No, I
insisted, now.

She must have thought I was an alcoholic. She kept trying to convince me that I had to wait until the plane was airborne, but I wasn't
going to budge. Needless to say, I couldn't tell anyone I was being deported. It was still a dangerous situation. You have to remember that
the enemy could have been on that plane as well, anywhere.

Suddenly I felt a man a few seats away staring at me. One of those
situations where you don't look up but you feel the person's eyes on you.
And for whatever reason, I began to laugh. I must have seemed like an

alcoholic and crazy to boot. He chuckled too, and I wanted to get a glimpse of the guy; I guess I expected to see someone looking like an undercover agent.

Aye, the twists of fate. It was my ex-husband's best friend, someone I hadn't run into for nine years. He took one look at me and began treating me as if I were disturbed. Of course I was gaunt looking, in terrible shape. He must have thought I'd spent the week in Honduras drinking. I'm no sooner seated on the plane than I'm asking the flight attendant for a double whiskey. Begging her, really. The guy looked at me, and he had an expression of pity on his face. Then he came over and took the seat beside me.

I had to spend that entire flight talking absurdities with this man: Have you seen so and so? How's so and so doing? The whole string of business people who were my husband's friends. There I was, with what I had just been through eating me up inside, needing to talk about it with someone, and I was forced to sustain a meaningless conversation like that one all the way from Honduras to Costa Rica. An hour and a half.

What's more, I didn't have a cent on me. So, to my further humiliation, when we landed I had to invent a story. You know, I told my ex-husband's friend I was robbed. Someone took my handbag. Could you give me twenty cents so I can call home? All this time, the guy never asked me if I was an alcoholic, but that's what he must have been thinking, I could tell. Even though I hadn't touched the drink I'd asked for. He offered to drive me home, but that's where I drew the line. So he gave me the twenty cents and I called home.

Two women friends happened to be at my house at the time. One of them was organized, the other not. Someone had called these two women from Honduras. Somehow they'd heard that something had happened to me, and they had gotten together to talk about what to do, how to proceed.

These two friends picked me up, they looked at me, they touched me, all the time asking: Are you all right? They thought I had suffered some sort of accident. That's when I told them: No, it wasn't an accident. I was captured and disappeared. Their reaction was very interesting. I assured them that physically I was all right, and the first thing they asked was if I wanted to see a gynecologist, to find out if I was pregnant. They simply assumed I'd been raped.

And of course it wasn't an idle assumption; women know about torture. But I told them: No, I wasn't raped. And the truth is, I don't want to go to a doctor right now. Let's sit down. I want to tell you what happened. I really needed to talk to someone. Because with Nora and the others, when we were released, we did talk some but it was fragmented. I needed to talk to someone totally removed from the situation in Honduras. And I told those two women everything. They listened, astonished.

Telling my story was very important, very very important. At the same time, I knew I wasn't going to be able to report what had happened. Once again we're faced with mandate and transgression. Why? Well I knew very well that the comrades weren't going to let me make public what I'd been through. At that time the clandestine structures were such that you just didn't report such events. You'd lose your cover if you did.

And for whatever reason, I myself didn't really want to make an official report of what had happened. Because I knew I could also lose my public persona. For the organization I was considered a clandestine cadre—I was doing underground work—but I also functioned above ground in significant ways. And I didn't want to lose either condition. If you were only clandestine, you had to go completely undercover. If you were only a public figure, you practically had to sever all ties with the organization. And I didn't want to be forced into either of those situations.

So I never did report what I'd been through. I've actually shared my story with almost no one, up until now. To give you an idea, in January when I brought Jennifer Harbury to CODEHUCA, to speak with the people with whom I've worked for five whole years, men and women with whom I've shared the utmost confidences, and Jennifer started explaining how she was gathering testimonies from those who had survived disappearance, I said—in front of those colleagues—that I was going to give my testimony to Jennifer Harbury as well.

This was just this past January. By that time Nora and I had found one another again, in October, in Managua. You'd done your first interview with us, and we'd agreed to do this book. And when I told those old friends and colleagues that I'd been disappeared fourteen years before, they were stunned. They'd worked with me for five years and knew nothing.

I myself had been one of the disappeared. And I'd worked for five years on behalf of the disappeared in all the countries of the region, and they never knew that. What I'm saying is that my encounter with Nora and with you, and our decision to tell our story, to publicly denounce what was done to us, means breaking a fifteen-year silence.[4]

There's the issue of silence itself, which is where I still have a lot of work to do. And there's the problem of guilt: How can you talk about yourself when you survived?

I wanted to ask you about that. You weren't murdered. You weren't raped. When so many others, the vast majority of the disappeared throughout Latin America, didn't survive. That must have made it even harder.

That's right. And we women are so good at working on behalf of others and not including ourselves. And with regard to the events in Honduras, my name never appeared in any of the solidarity communiqués—for obvious reasons, which I've already explained. So it was even easier for me not to speak.

I lived through the ensuing years as if I were a mirror for others—as one of the ordinary women prisoners I was working with last week told me—and no one even knew why I was a mirror.

How terrible. I don't know how you survived those years of silence. You know, I understand how you managed to survive the nine days of imprisonment, of torture, but I don't understand how you survived the silence—I mean survived it without going mad. I understand the physical survival because people do what they have to do to make it through. Women are particularly good at this. But I don't know how you got through the aftermath without falling apart. You've been able to keep this buried to a large extent, while at the same time continuing to develop as someone who values women's voices, the sharing of our stories, the enormous source of strength in that.

I think I was able to get through that, to a great extent, because of my clandestine training. There were so many silences. And we had to learn to live with them. But you know, Margaret, this experience also leads me to question some of the analyses we accept, those essentially bipolar analyses, the assessment that women just naturally do everything for others and nothing for ourselves. I don't think this is natural to our condition.

Because, listen, I went to work at the Commission on Human Rights not because I was ordered to do so, not because that was my political work as others saw it, but because I had to. I had to become an expert in human rights, an expert in disappearance. Why did I feel that I had to do this kind of work? Of course it had to do with popular education, educating people about what was going on. But there was something else . . .

You needed a venue in which you could talk about what you'd been through without having to personalize the experience. In speaking of other people's cases you were able to unleash some of the rage, the fear, the questions— you were able to help expose what was going on without having to talk about your own case.

Precisely. And that's exactly what made it possible for me to survive. But, but, what made it possible for me to finally speak out, even though it is fifteen years later, was my experience with FIRE. Because at FIRE we give voice to those who have no voice. In order to speak, without censure, about absolutely everything. At FIRE I'd recorded the voices of so many women, I'd broken their silences with them, and I'd done this with and for everyone but myself.

In 1987, five years after the experience, I was fortunate to be able to work with a therapist who knew the Central American context. She had also been a victim of certain traumas—different, but similar in some ways. The therapist I went to had been involved in the struggle in El Salvador. She'd studied with Jesuits and had participated in the demonstration at the San Salvador cathedral in 1976. She just happened to leave that demonstration in order to breast-feed her baby, five blocks away. When she returned, everyone was dead.

This woman's personal history also included an experience of repression and of escaping with her life when so many others didn't. She understood that kind of guilt firsthand. In spite of the fact that she didn't specialize in post-traumatic stress disorder, she did know something about the issues. In that therapy, I dealt with trying to separate mandate and transgression—the voices that come from inside and those that seem to come from out there. I learned to identify those voices, to understand where they were really coming from. The therapy helped me a great deal to affirm myself in certain areas.

Then, much more recently, some four years ago, I did a year of psychodrama. Group therapy. It was once a week. At that point I was dealing mostly with organizational issues, my political militancy, my relationships with other women on the Left, my lesbianism in that context. This was also a very important issue for me to work through. So those have been my two periods of psychotherapy.

Another thing that's been important in all this has been my experience of the duality between life and death. I think I was able to live through the ordeal in Honduras with a certain degree of calm precisely because I never believed they were going to kill me. Not even when I was on the front lines in El Salvador. I was there for four years and never thought I was going to die. This comes from a certain naiveté as well as a deep sense of self-preservation.

It was interesting, in our first interview in Managua, the difference between you and Nora in this respect. She was sure she was going to die, and you were sure you weren't.

That's right. And it wasn't until I went with Nora to talk to the special attorney general, just the night before last in Tegucigalpa, that I really understood what they'd had planned for us. I couldn't sleep last night, thinking about it. The special attorney general, with documents that have turned up, confirmed the fact that indeed we were all supposed to have been murdered. A thread of icy blood ran through my body when I heard that—the same sensation I'd had back then, when they had us in those prisons.

What do you think prevented them from shooting you? Protest from the solidarity community, government pressure, what?

The voices of protest. And also my own case. As a foreigner, as a Costa Rican, shooting me would have meant repercussions they couldn't gauge at the time. In fact I realized this toward the end of the time in captivity. They told me I was free to leave, but I knew that if I left, my comrades—Nora and the others—would be shot. It was very clear to me. So I refused to leave until they freed us all.

That took a great deal of courage.

It was the only thing to do.

María, tell me a little more about those moments in the special attorney general's office. You said you had the same sensation you'd experienced fifteen years before, the thread of ice-cold blood running through your body. That body sensation interests me a great deal.

Well, there had been a moment during my captivity when they came and threatened to rape me, and another when they carried out a mock execution. Both times I felt as if a thread of icy blood was running through my body. I'd never had that sensation before. It was my response to the threat of death—be it from rape or from the firing squad. And I've never experienced the sensation since. It's a feeling of pure panic. It's also a biological response I think. I'm not sure, because I haven't studied these things, but it seems to me to be panic in its most physical manifestation. What you feel in your veins at that moment is freezing cold. And you feel it as if it were the vein itself, freezing.

But I also think that this physical reaction actually changes your body temperature and provides you with a momentary sense of calm. A sense of great calm, actually. Because I was able, at those moments, to compose myself and respond appropriately—with the only weapon I had, which was my voice. And so I managed to keep from passing out, to remain upright before the expected bullet hit.

I believe there's a physical aspect to all this, because I don't think one's physical state reflects one's mental or emotional state alone. That great feeling of calm. I've seen few people die, but you often hear about that sudden calm before a person dies. People talk about that calm. I think it must be a chemical response, that feeling of coldness followed by calm, in the moments between knowing you are about to die and dying.

The other day when Nora and I were with the special attorney general and she produced that document and I once again experienced the reaction I'd had fifteen years before, it almost undid me. I couldn't sleep that night. It wasn't until the next morning that I was able to talk to my colleagues about what I'd experienced. They knew I was going to the special attorney general's office with Nora. And they knew the visit would probably affect me deeply.

But you know, Margaret, I sometimes wonder how this sort of thing works, exactly. I mean, if this sort of reaction doesn't also respond to the capacity we have—or perhaps the capacity I in particular have—of delaying emotional response. It's as if your emotions enter into a delayed reaction mode. And I have this capacity. Sometimes it turns out to be a survival skill.

I think it's very common, especially with a certain type of woman: that ability, in a moment of crisis, to put feelings aside. You don't allow yourself to really absorb what's happening. And that's how you keep on going. Intellectually you follow what's happening, but emotionally you delay your reaction. Then, later, you may go to pieces.

María, what I would like you to do now is to think about four words: memory, body, voice, and choice. I'd like you to think about these four words in relation to your own life, to specific moments in your life in which two or more of these words have intersected.

I have it! The minute you said voice and choice, I knew I wanted to tell you this story. And it's the first story I recorded for Feminist International Radio Endeavor, when I began the project in 1991. It's the story of when I was maybe six or seven years old and I used to say bad words left and right. It was a logical result of the ambiguities I lived: on the one hand, having to learn to be a woman, and on the other, sensing my mother's contradictions with having given birth to a girl. I learned all these words from the boys I played with, and I used to swear all over the place. And my mother, in particular, began to become very concerned about this. I would cuss in school, anywhere.

My mother always told me that with me she tried to use my own inclinations, but move them in a different direction. I guess she knew there was no use fighting the tide; out and out confrontation wasn't going to get her anywhere with me. And being a teacher, she decided that once she had gone through the list of traditional methods—like punishing me by putting me in my bedroom when I said a bad word, things like that, which of course only had the effect of making me say more such words—at a certain point she decided that she was going to try her own teaching methods.

So she sat me in front of her, and she said: look, you can say the ten worst words you can think of. Say them out loud. But I'm going to teach you how to listen to yourself as you do that.

I was fascinated, you know? Here I was being given the opportunity, or the permission, or the mandate, or whatever you want to call it, to say the ten worst words in front of my mother and not get punished for it! Then she said: but before you begin I'm going to teach you how to listen to yourself. And she took one of my hands in hers and placed it over my ear, covered it, you know how musicians do, and then she told me I could begin with the words.

I began: *mierda, puta, coño*[5]. . . all those bad words, very loud, and of course with her hand and mine over my ear. And then, when I had finished, I just sighed. I was waiting for the hot pepper or the scolding or whatever, you know, and she just looked at me and asked: Did you hear yourself? I told her yes. And she asked me: What did you hear? And I just looked at her. And then I said: the anger, the anger because I'm not allowed to be myself!

What I said when I recorded this story for the radio was that feminist radio is giving back to woman the importance of her own voice. And giving back to a woman the importance of her voice is giving her back the importance of her life. Then at the end of this story, I talked about how, when I was a child and had that experience with my mother, when I was able to actually listen to myself, I was able to hear not only the words themselves but the anger that was their source.

And then at the very end I said: Doing feminist radio is having one ear open to listen to others and the other closed to listen to what's inside yourself. That's what feminist radio is all about. One ear closed and the other open. But I don't think we can make the connections, not really, until we are able to separate the voices. That's my perspective. Why we sometimes cannot make the connections isn't because we're not smart or whatever, but because we cannot separate the voices. Not only other women's voices, but the voices—the mandates—we have ingrained in ourselves.

Because if I listen to you, I can identify only if I accept, recognize, and am able to hear you and your experience. I may understand that mine is related. But if I listen to your voice and feel it's mine, then there's not necessarily a connection. Do you know what I mean?

That's a very interesting distinction. And it's one I've really never heard before. Why do you think it is, María, that if we just automatically identify, we don't get it? If we identify without making that distinction. Do you think it might be because we have this habit—and I believe it's a habit that is deeply conditioned from our earliest years—that when we are listening to someone else, we're almost always also thinking of what we're going to say in response? And thus not really listening?

That's one part. Another, perhaps the hardest, is what I learned when my mother did her experiment with me. It is claiming our own voice and learning how to listen to it. We have been taught to validate everybody's voice but our own. To listen to everybody but ourselves.

And to trust other people's voices more than we trust our own . . .

Yes, even to trust other people's voice, pitch, tone, content, rather than our own. So if you ask me what the main thing about the ability to separate these voices is, I'd say that only when we separate can we really listen to our own. You know, the most difficult thing about doing radio with women, and the thing I like best, is that women not only get to share their voices by putting them on the tape recorder, but they also sit there and listen to themselves. Sometimes for the first time. We can't take it. And it's so empowering when we give ourselves permission to listen to ourselves. That's when you really begin to appreciate the worth, the strength, the pain!

I never use one of those microphones you put on the table. One, because they're very expensive. Even if I interview seven women at a time. It's like the Indian talking stick. When you use a single microphone, you have to separate the voices. One woman talks and the others have to listen to her. When I am holding the microphone, I can talk and listen to myself.

Getting back to memory, body, voice, and choice for a moment, I wonder if you could talk to me a bit about how coordinating FIRE has changed your life, your perspective. I'd like you to try to reflect on the connections you've been able to make in your personal life. Because the political work is absolutely astounding. Very very impressive. And of course it's all connected. But I think we tend to talk less about the other. And as much as I want the political issues to be central to this book, I also want to make these other connections.

Well, first of all, I think that having the power that comes with holding a microphone—making that accessible to my own voice and to other women's voices—is an almost limitless act of mirroring. When I use the term *mirroring* what I mean is the act of listening to oneself and to others and being able to separate the voices. That's when you make the meaningful connections.

I have seen myself, experienced myself, in almost every testimony I have recorded throughout these years of FIRE. Women in such diverse countries, such diverse situations. By now I've been all over the world, you know. And it's not just about having been all over the world but about having all that diversity come on the air, making it accessible to so many other women.

It's been amazing. You have to understand that when I began working at FIRE, my experience over the previous fifteen years had been very grass roots, very local, and focalized you know, and all of a sudden I was running this international shortwave radio.[6] Or it was running me! These were the voices I'd hardly ever had access to before.

And here I was with this instrument in my hand, and I was listening to woman after woman after woman, receiving tapes from all over the world, with amazing perspectives that I had never heard before. Before FIRE I hadn't been able to listen to these women from other countries.

I think we get caught up in models or in formulas. I know that as someone who for years had heard about the Salvadoran struggle—for us in the United States, or even in Nicaragua, where I lived for a time—the idea of a struggle in which 25 percent of the leadership positions had to be held by women, or more at some levels, sounded extraordinary to me. And to other women I knew. We talked about it with admiration. The model sounded superb. And then to find out that it was still relatively meaningless. I guess we don't stop to think about what happens when these well-publicized models translate into real-life situations.

That's exactly right. And going back to what you asked me, how FIRE has also reshaped my life, my way of being, I think the most important thing is that I have been able to dialogue with the broadest possible diversity. And especially, as I said, the issue of being able to separate the voices. In order to make the connections. That's a skill that has re-shaped the way in which I interact with practically everyone.

I'd like to be able to go more deeply into this particular aspect, the separation of self from other, other from self. You've mentioned this so many times, and you've approached explaining it. But I'm not sure you've really explained it as fully as you might.

I'm very interested in this, not only because I've never heard it addressed in just this way before, but because in fact we are bogged down by theoreticians of all stripes who constantly talk about how we must identify with one another, become one, that sort of thing. In the arena of personal relationships this is always something that astounds me. When I hear someone say we have become one. As if that were a good thing. That seems to me to be a recipe for disaster.

It's an affirmation of identity and diversity. Because if I listen to you talking about an experience that I relate to, and I cannot hear your voice as separate from my own, I will be able to make a connection that will bring us closer together but I will never be able to appreciate you for your own experience, your own identity, your own history, your own context. And I will lose out.

I think I have it very clear. And this is true especially in journalism, as a communicator. Journalists can identify but never appreciate the wholeness of the other person's experience. As women we share something profound. But we also come from a whole series of very different contexts. One of the main issues here, I think, is subjectivity. Only searching for our commonalities, without being able to separate speaker and listener, leads to a kind of abstraction in which subjectivity is lost.

My history—as a woman born in Puerto Rico, in 1948, middle class, in a family that expected a boy instead of a girl, all of that—my personal history is not only shaped by these events; it's not the same as my sisters', for example. And if I am not able to separate this, I'm not able to appreciate the full dimension of who a woman is. The connection may be good, but it's partial.

This is so important. I don't know if what you're talking about has any bearing on what's happening with feminists in Central America, but it has tremendous bearing on what's been happening in the U.S. women's movement in this last decade of the twentieth century. We've had community after community ripped apart over the issue of racism. Difference. And the ideas that women have about diversity. Much of what you've been saying speaks to this.

How does one really understand diversity? How do we live with one another? How are we able to really see and hear a sister from a totally different cultural context? And of course this includes race, economics, sexual identification, age, degree of abilities, the whole range. How can we internalize another woman's experience? There's that sense of: oh, we've got to identify with so and so or such and such. But we can't, not really. I can't really identify with you as a Puerto Rican, coming from a colonialist culture, who went to religious schools, who became a nun, who worked in the liberated zones of El Salvador for four years. I may want to, but how can I?

Unless you make such an abstraction that I'm no longer there.

Right. And on top of this there are also the other overlays, ways in which we can identify. But that's not the problematic part. I can admire you, I can sympathize with you, I can study you. I can try to question and challenge myself in relation to your experience: in what ways have I absorbed the colonialism of my own society, for example.

For that you have to listen to yourself, not to me. That's exactly what I'm talking about. That's the separation I'm talking about. You know, I'm working with these ideas right now with a male friend of mine— around his prison experience. He was one of the early comrades taken prisoner in El Salvador, and the only one who survived. And he was able to survive because in some way or other he managed to negotiate. He was terribly tortured. And his subsequent silence has damaged him too.

We spoke last night as a matter of fact. He seems ready to talk about his experience now, but like a turtle who sticks his head out of his shell and then quickly draws it back in again. By now I think we have enough of a relationship so that he might be able to engage in this process. He's the husband of one of my best friends. He wants to write; he's been wanting to do that for twenty years and hasn't been able to. This man was able to survive because he was able to find ways of negotiating with his torturers and with the guards. And the Left accused him of treason.

When he got out of prison, he was totally isolated. The torture itself had traumatized him, but the rejection and isolation traumatized him even more. I think he may be ready now, and that I can help him. It's his process, but I feel that I can be there for him. I know I can be his mirror.

The political context was so either/or in those years, so severe. Either you betrayed or you didn't. You passed the test or you didn't. There was no middle ground.

This issue of interactive autonomy and negotiation is important. We need to talk about this and develop it as much as possible. I think it's very relevant.

You know, María, for the past hour or so you've been speaking in English. I know you know this; I'm not telling you anything you don't know. But I'm wondering how comfortable it is for you. I certainly don't want to ask you to speak in English. I want you to speak in the language that's most comfortable.

I know. And that's why . . . Well, this is also an interesting issue. Maybe we can talk about the reasons I believe I switch from one language to the other, the subjects I tend to express in Spanish and those I express in English.

The fact is I stopped speaking English for seventeen years, after I came to Costa Rica, and while I was in El Salvador and Nicaragua. And then, all of a sudden, here I was with this radio show, and I'm the producer of the English program. After seventeen years of not using my English! This has also had an impact on me. I've been able to get back into my English, not just because I've had to for the radio but because of the many English-speaking women I've listened to—and their many different kinds of English.

Maybe I began speaking in English when we began to talk about FIRE. Right?

That's right, you did. So let's explore this a bit more. Negotiation and language. Two good subjects.

The language you speak at one time or another has so much to do with the language you associate with particular feelings. Or experiences.

I understand what you're saying. For me, giving birth has been in Spanish; anything having to do with raising my children—that's Spanish. My Marxism is in Spanish. But my feminism and my lesbianism are in English. My incest work is in English. So for me it's very much about the feelings. But it's also about the experiences. Which parts of my life were lived in one language or the other.

Yes. And this is so relevant to what they call multiculturalism. I know people who are multicultural, and others who are monocultural even though they may have lived in a dozen different countries.

For a while I'd been noticing a black cord around María's neck, from which four small and variable-sized brass fish hung. I'd wondered if these fish have a meaning and had been waiting for the moment to ask. Now I do ask, and María's eyes fill with delight as she acknowledges the question.

My mother gave this necklace to me last year. She's a fisherwoman, I've told you that. She's a fisherwoman and so am I. Last year I asked my mother to write the story of when I came back from El Salvador and saw my parents after four years of almost no contact. I had nieces and nephews I didn't even know about!

I went home. And, you know, my relationship with my mother has always been somewhat confrontational: I do what I want to do, and you stay clear of that! You can involve yourself in anything else, but not my life. But this time I was so happy to be there, to see them! The day I arrived I said to her: you know, Mom, tomorrow I will do with you—or you can do with me—whatever you want. You decide.

She almost died! She didn't know what to say. And she didn't really know what she wanted. Because she was used to having to convince me whenever she wanted us to do something together. After the surprise had passed, she said: well, let us register to be the only two fisherwomen in the sailfish tournament! It's tomorrow. Let's go fishing together, as a team.

Now mind you, I was coming from El Salvador, in the middle of the war, and here I had made this commitment to my mother. I was committed to doing whatever she asked. But I needed to be very low-key in Puerto Rico, very discreet; I really didn't want anyone to know I was there. Because I still didn't know how things were going to work out, if I was going to be able to go back to El Salvador. And now I was going to have to go and register for this asshole, elitist fishing tournament!

The yachts and all that. Of course our boat wasn't that big. My brother was going to be the captain, and he had the smallest boat in the tournament. He's a very good fisherman, and my mother and I are also very good fisherwomen. I thought, well, I told her anything she wanted. Here I am, and this is what we're going to do.

I think this may have been the first time I broke with always being so disciplined, acting on principle. I was going to do something for a totally different reason. Something I'd wanted to do for a while. So we went and registered. And I won't tell you the whole story. I'll just say that we ended up being the only two fisherpersons in that tournament who caught sailfish and won awards. My mother caught two sailfish and I caught two. We ended up winning all the awards, which was devastating for the rest of the participants.

But the press was there too, all kinds of press. And I had this hat, in the pictures, which I pulled way down, trying to cover my face. All in all, it was an amazing experience. And then I understood what she had wanted to do. Of course we didn't know we were going to win. She didn't know that either: half of it is luck and half is skill. But it was such an amazing experience, that I asked her to write about it. I have some great pictures, of us getting the awards and so on. And some funny stories, because most of the prizes were certificates to buy clothing at men's stores. . . . There was a bouquet of flowers for the *dama destacada* (distinguished lady)—which of course we also won!—but it's really meant for the fishermen's wives. You know, they get a little something! It was all so unbelievable. And it was the first shared experience that my mother and I were able to analyze from a feminist perspective.

So, getting back to these fish; I don't know why or how it happened; but the thing is, when I asked my mother to write this story—and she began to write and she got very nervous, because she was worried about how my brother, who had been the captain of our boat, would interpret it. She said: I really can't write about this yet. I have to work on it some more, find a way of writing it, because I'm afraid that he's going to get angry. . . .

The next day we went shopping together, and she saw these fish at GAP. She said: I'm going to buy these for you. And she put them around my neck.

And now that you mention this necklace, I remember that we caught four fish that day. She caught two and I caught two. So I'm sure this is one of those coincidences that aren't coincidences. She probably didn't notice this either.

That's a great story. Now if I remember correctly, we were going to explore a bit more, or you were going to explore the issue of negotiation. Do you have anything else you want to say about negotiation?

I think I said all I could about negotiation. Maybe what's left is interactive autonomy, as a basis for negotiation. We've talked a great deal about autonomy, but I feel that in the history of the movement— as well as in our individual histories—we've talked about autonomy because we've had to gather ourselves separately from men. This is woman's great drama: finding a way to separate ourselves, to see ourselves as individuals and to be able to relate to others from that position of wholeness.

When you say separate, do you mean separate ourselves from men, and also from our families of origin, from our . . .

Yes, from the mandates, everything. And I think that feminism has done a good enough job of proposing autonomy. What we have to do now, from this position of autonomy, is to learn to affect society as a whole. We have to learn anew how to make alliances, how to relate to others. Because, as you know, those years in which we learned to separate ourselves were years of tremendous rupture.

I'm talking about the history of feminism without claiming that we've all lived exactly the same process. It's a general characteristic, historically speaking. Today's challenge, for me, is to learn how to become interactively autonomous, to not relinquish our autonomy but still to be able to interact, relate, build alliances. We have to be able to create these alliances without losing our hard-won autonomy, which is the other side of the drama.

Some of us have decided to call this new state that we want to develop interactive autonomy, because of course autonomy is also relative. Only when we are at the margin does autonomy seem to be complete. At the margin of a relationship, at the margin of another social group, at the margin of public politics. . . . So for us the real interactive autonomy must be that from which we can reaffirm our objectives, our interests, our needs, our identities, but with the ability to relate, to struggle with others—men as well as women.

The other thing at this stage of the game is that the idea of women's autonomy is very threatening. It doesn't say anything about what we want. We have to build bridges. Our autonomy doesn't say anything positive to others. The idea is not simply threatening because the power structure doesn't believe that women have the right to be autonomous, but because the term itself doesn't express the fact that we're neither looking for marginalization nor interested in marginalizing others. So, for me, the concept of interactive autonomy is this: the strategies, the forms by which, from an autonomous position, we can work again with others. We need to integrate our questions, our issues, our arenas of struggle. For this reason some of us here don't use the word *autonomy* anymore without its first name: interactive.

This issue is very important for us right now, as feminists, as members of a women's movement, and also as individual women at the end of the twentieth century.[7] The term expresses what we're looking for much better than simple autonomy. We've been influenced by the language of computers, and we use this terminology a bit in jest—and also so we'll be understood by the younger feminists who have grown up in the computer age, who don't know our history. These younger women have grown up without the trauma of autonomy versus subjugation. They walk on the bridges we built, without being able to name them as such.

If you look at the history of feminism in Central America—and you of all people know that history well—it's a feminist movement that was forced to break with the Left. Not everyone, of course, but the vast majority of the women. Most of us belonged to mixed organizations on the Left. Our struggles originated in those organizations. And so many of us—as with my own history—had to break with those organizations, with work that meant a great deal to us, in order to find our own identities.

In Nicaragua, in Guatemala, in El Salvador, in Honduras. And in Costa Rica. Almost all of us, feminists in these countries, have our roots in the Left. Even if every Central American feminist doesn't come out of a Left organization, the roots of the feminist movement as a whole are there. And the drama of our autonomy, with respect to the Left, has been major.

We had to break with our own belief systems. Because it wasn't that we stopped being socialists, we didn't stop being progressive, we didn't stop being leftists, we didn't stop believing that feminism has to be part of the struggle for social transformation—for all of us, men and women alike. We had to break with the Left because we weren't being considered in the Left's projects, and because we didn't have any real voice or power we couldn't change things from within. Believe me, we tried.

Autonomy was our drama of the 1980s and 1990s. In each of the Central American countries, almost simultaneously, an autonomous feminist movement emerged. Independent of the Left, and independent of much else. But none of us advocated for a feminism only about women's rights. We were always very clear that we were struggling for social justice—for everyone. From the beginning, we tried to build bridges, connections, proposals that could be inserted into the overall struggle.

Today's drama, in our region, is our search for interactive autonomy. Central America is not that different from other regions, from other countries, in this respect. Particularly with the problem of globalization. No proposal that takes into account a single gender, no sectorial proposal of any kind, really makes sense anymore. We have to make meaningful alliances with other sectors, with other groups, sometimes even with people in government, with international organizations and so forth.

Some of our organizations are born autonomous, but we always have this tendency to give away our power. Power and authority. And we get our power from different places. In general, we get our moral power from being women: our capacity for work, the justice of what we propose and do. Neither money nor control of the means of communication has been our strong point. And these are two things that are absolutely central to the exercise of power, to the structure of power. It's been very important for us to process this.

SEVEN

WHEN I LOOK INTO THE MIRROR
AND SEE YOU

A small news item reported by the Associated Press caught my eye just as I was finishing this book: "More Bodies Found at Contra Base" announced the *New York Times* headline on August 31, 2001. I began to read:

> Tegucigalpa, Honduras (AP)—After days of intense digging, forensic researchers have uncovered the remains of fifteen people in a former U.S. base used to train the Nicaraguan Contras in the 1980s.
>
> Working under the watchful eye of human rights groups and local prosecutors, the researchers began their search at El Aguacate air base on Monday and will continue digging for a total of twenty days. They will conduct laboratory analyses until the end of September.
>
> The federal prosecutor's office expects to find the remains of as many as 80 of 185 leftists who disappeared between 1979 and 1990. Human rights groups say some of the disappeared were tortured and buried at the base.
>
> The United States built El Aguacate in 1984 as a training center for the Contras, who were fighting the leftist Sandinista regime in neighboring Nicaragua during the 1980s. The base is located near the border of the two countries, about 80 miles east of Tegucigalpa.
>
> It was turned over to the Honduran military before being abandoned in 1994.
>
> . . . The list of missing people includes 105 Hondurans, 39 Nica-

raguans, 28 Salvadorans, five Costa Ricans, four Guatemalans, two U.S. citizens, an Ecuadorian and a Venezuelan.

As has so often been true in the past, years of anguished search have given way to an event that may bring closure to some of the families of the disappeared. Some of the voiceless will be given voice, at least insofar as the whereabouts of their bodies are concerned. Once again, proof of U.S. complicity will have been established. This discovery is the result of tireless, often tedious work on the part of families and human rights workers who refused to accept the official story. Bearing witness takes many forms.

But the general picture remains the same. Closure will have come too late. The anguish of not knowing will remain for others. The guilty, if they face justice at all, will get off with little or no punishment for their crimes. Most of the masterminds are long gone or continue to enjoy the immunity endowed by authoritarian privilege. The recent attempt to bring Chilean ex-president Augusto Pinochet to trial and the trials of those such as Slobodan Milosivec in The Hague indicate a new willingness on the part of some sectors to bring the guilty to justice. But for the most part impunity rules.

History also seems doomed to repeat itself. Even when the horror of these crimes is laid bare and U.S. involvement amply documented, few seem to draw comparisons with current atrocities elsewhere. Stories become circumscribed to a particular place at a particular time. The lessons remain unlearned.

At a more personal level, though, the stories hold a meaning that cannot be erased. Through the telling and the listening, women especially are weaving a new recipe for life.

There are the women.

There are the stories.

There are the mirrors that reflect the stories.

And there are the ways in which women especially interpret these stories, what we choose to do with them.

After their release, Nora told her parents what she had been through.

Her parents tried to listen, although her father in particular was only able to allow a few of the horrendous details in. María told a couple of friends who were at her San José apartment when she returned from Honduras. But she was unable to share her story with her family or any of her closest friends and colleagues until many years later. Both women, although their respective jobs involved bearing witness to similar stories of other women's lives, were reluctant to tell their own.

Fourteen years of relative silence — or silences — required an elaborate set of circumstances to be unlocked. Some of these circumstances were products of a different historical moment. Some had to be constructed, created at great personal cost. But silence was no longer an option. The pain of the telling had become preferable to the pain of silence, which had become unbearable. Both speaker and listener had to step up to a different equation. A new sort of mirror.

One of the most painful lessons we have learned from the failures of our recent past is that future strategies must make space for personal as well as organizational health. All groups and individuals have an inalienable right to wholeness; all human experience must be honored.

When we look into the mirror and see something besides our own face staring back, it is because we have prepared ourselves to see more. Literally fought through the barrage of corporate lies in order to see differently, to truly see. To do this, it is necessary to clean our senses of the thick layer of interference quite intentionally fabricated to bind our senses and our knowing.

As María tells us, we must learn to listen to others and to listen to ourselves. Then we must learn to separate the voices.

The official story — the story constructed of voices and images, sounds and subliminal insistence — has all but taken over in today's society. We are so overly saturated with the sounds (loud, ear-cracking, soul-numbing), the images (youthful, thin, competitive, rich, the thoughtless and self-indulgent constantly held up for emulation), the messages (you need that home, car, or cruise — their acquisition will make you happier or more successful), and the political lies (the idea that the United States government supports democracy at home or around the world), that we have forgotten how to look differently, how to listen for the real stories. They, and therefore we ourselves, are weighed down by vested interests, which we have learned to accept without question.

Today's official story belies confirmation on many counts. Sometimes we are able to take it apart and examine those pieces that pretend to reflect our own experience. We may at least be able to acknowledge our unfamiliarity with those pieces; we may even understand they are lies. This requires a certain amount of thoughtfulness. Sometimes it requires courage.

Calling the whole story's bluff is more difficult. It requires greater risk. Doing so may be unpopular, even dangerous, at this time when patriotism is equated with conformity and the power of might makes right would seem to obliterate independent analysis, and choice.

To look into the mirror and see all life, the histories of all living beings as well as our own, we may almost need to begin again.

For women and for all those who are marginalized by the white, male, upper-class power structure, this is complex. For we must first make the shift from margin to center—the psychological shift, the emotional shift, a shift of the senses as well as of information.

Nothing helps us make this shift more effectively than telling and listening to our real stories, assimilating their experiences, learning their lessons. For it is in our stories that the power lies, a power capable of disentangling and deconstructing those mechanisms one group has maintained for so long in order to control the others.

Nora and María shared their interactive mirror with me. I share it here with you. And I ask you to remember that however extraordinary this testimony is, we all have stories that, if spoken and heard, hold truths that can change our lives.

Each of us is capable of seeing herself in another's face.

NOTES

ONE   THE PRISM: WOMEN'S HUMAN RIGHTS

1. Since the 1970s, in the United States and Europe, feminist language took care to specifically include women. This practice came later in Latin America, but since the mid-1990s, innovations in spoken and written Spanish recognize women as a distinct group. Because Spanish is a gendered language, the change presented interesting challenges. Today Latin American feminists and their supporters easily say *las* and *los* (hers and his), and when writing they often use the @ (which looks like an *a* and an *o* combined) at the end of a pronoun to indicate reference to both men and women.

2. In Buenos Aires, Argentina, a special maternity unit existed in one of the dictatorship's detention centers, intended specifically to harvest the babies of imprisoned women who were pregnant.

3. One such case is that of Norma Arrostito, member of the Argentinean Montoneras, who was captured and held at the ESMA (Escuela de Mecánica de la Armada) during that country's brutal dictatorship. Arrostito couldn't be broken in the torture sessions, so her captors fed her well, dressed her elegantly, and placed her behind a desk in the institution's front offices. There, prohibited from speaking, she served as a sinister warning to anyone who entered; the well-known revolutionary had apparently gone over to the other side. When no longer of use, Arrostito was disappeared.

4. Statement reviewing the Vienna Declaration and Programme of Action (VDPA) on behalf of hundreds of organizations from around the

world participating in the 1998 Global Campaign for Women's Human Rights.

5. Ibid.

6. Maren Ulriksen de Viñar, ed., *Memoria social: Fragmentaciones y responsabilidades* (Montevideo, Uruguay: Ediciones Trilce, 2001), 9.

TWO   NORA AND MARÍA

1. Caritas is a Catholic relief organization, with offices throughout the developing world.

2. Several months before Nora and María met in Managua, Honduras's new civilian government was forced to open legal proceedings against the torturers of the previous decade. Nora had decided to make her claim before this newly appointed tribunal and so had been looking for María to be a witness in her case.

3. Carlos Fonseca was the founder and maximum leader of the Sandinista National Liberation Front (FSLN) until his death in 1976. Presumably this prisoner, in his delirium, was invoking his name.

4. Several months after this interview took place, the process that had momentarily opened up in Honduras closed once more. It was all a smoke screen, was the way Nora put it.

5. W.O.M.E.N. sponsored a cultural evening, when different members of the delegation read poetry or sang to one another. Some of our Nicaraguan friends also participated. Two South African women, Nomboniso Gasa and Gertrude Fester, recited poetry they had written about their prison experiences during the years of apartheid.

6. Fempress was a women's news service that existed, first in Mexico and then in Chile, for almost twenty years (1980s and 1990s). With permanent correspondents in fourteen Latin American countries, it produced a magazine, periodic press releases, radio broadcasts, and finally a web site where more than a thousand articles can still be accessed. One of Fempress's enduring successes is its handbook, *The ABCs of Non-Sexist Journalism.*

7. Marcela Lagarde is a Mexican feminist psychotherapist whose work has been particularly helpful to Latin American women dealing with the scars of political and domestic abuse.

THREE   CENTRAL AMERICA: WHERE AND WHO?

1. I owe many of the statistics and some of the analysis quoted in this chapter to the Inter-Hemispheric Education Resource Center's guides to each country. The Inter-Hemispheric Education Resource Center can be contacted at P.O. Box 4506, Albuquerque, N.M. 87196.

2. Tom Barry, *Inside Guatemala* (Albuquerque: Inter-Hemispheric Resource Center, 1992), 95.

FOUR   DISAPPEARANCE

1. Because they consider the word *disappeared* to be too impersonal a term with which to describe this particular repressive act, Honduras's Commission for the Defense of Human Rights in Central America (CODEHUCA) suggests the use of *kidnapped* instead. Disappearance, according to CODEHUCA, most accurately reflects the reality for the family members left behind, because they cannot know what happened to their loved ones. It does not define the practice as political policy, nor the responsibility or methods used by those who carried out the crime of disappearance on such a massive scale. For the purpose of this book, however, I prefer to use the word *disappeared. Kidnapped* evokes the moment of capture, whereas *disappeared*—in my mind at least—implies an endless empty future in which a lack of closure around the victim's demise continues to plague his or her family, friends, and society at large.

2. Testimony about this and other events that took place during the years of the dictatorships in Uruguay and Argentina is from a series of conversations with Emilia Carlevaro, Uruguayan member of the Latin American Organization of the Families of the Disappeared, Montevideo, December 2001.

3. Sheila R. Tully, "A Painful Purgatory: Grief and the Nicaraguan Mothers of the Disappeared," *Social Science and Medicine* 40: 1597–1610.

4. This statistic of 185 conflicts with an earlier accepted statistic of 184. Another report of a disappeared person may have surfaced, or someone else may have been disappeared in more recent years.

5. For a good initial history of the mothers and grandmothers, see Jo Fisher, *Mothers of the Disappeared* (Boston: South End Press, 1989).

6. Gen. Augusto Pinochet, dictator of Chile for seventeen years, who

even after the restoration of democracy retains political immunity for life, was captured on a trip to London in the late 1990s. A Spanish judge had built a case against him for his involvement in crimes against Spanish citizens. Pinochet was held under house arrest in England for a number of months and finally returned to Chile, where it was promised that he would stand trial. Before he could do so, doctors declared him unfit and he was released. This attempt to bring the magna terrorists to justice, however, has had an impact on other perpetrators of genocide, who now think twice before traveling internationally.

7. Gary Cohn and Ginger Thompson, "Unearthed: Fatal Secrets," *Baltimore Sun,* June 11–18, 1995. This four-part series documents the fact that in Honduras, "hundreds of citizens were kidnapped, tortured and killed in the 1980s by a secret army trained and supported by the Central Intelligence Agency." This secret army was Battalion 316. Much of the material for the series came from interviews with three former Battalion 316 torturers who had escaped to Canada. They could no longer live with their own silence.

8. After a brutal coup ousted the Allende government on September 11, 1973, a nurse in one of Chile's military hospitals managed to smuggle out a photograph of the comatose disappeared revolutionary Bautista van Showen. Van Showen was also rumored to have told his captors: "You don't know why you torture me, but I know why I die."

9. After the 2001 terrorist attack on the World Trade Center, government agencies and private charities sought to address the needs of many but certainly not all of those victimized by the crime; the many undocumented workers who had worked at the twin towers were of course left unattended.

10. María Suárez Toro, *Women's Voices on Fire: Feminist International Radio Endeavor* (Austin, Tex.: Anomaly Press, 1999).

FIVE   NORA

1. Nora's husband, Renato, died of lung cancer about a year after this conversation was recorded. At the time of the interview, he had not yet been diagnosed.

SIX   MARÍA

1. The Second Vatican Council was called by Pope John XXIII in 1962. It

prescribed a gospel-oriented content for Catholicism and a more socially conscious doctrine than that of previous papal encyclicals, ecumenical dialogue with other denominations and with non-Christians, more responsibility for laypersons in the Church's pastoral work, and liturgical reforms that included the introduction of language, songs, and instruments native to different countries. When saying mass, priests no longer kept their backs to their congregations. In 1968, at the meeting of bishops in Medellín, Colombia, Vatican II found its Latin American application. The Church recognized institutional violence, colonial structures, economic dictatorships, and an "international imperialism of money." The result was liberation theology, which declared a "Church of the oppressed."

2. She would stop several days after this taping. Perhaps the self-examination helped conclude what had been an ongoing struggle.

3. The Farabundo Martí National Liberation Front (FMLN). Farabundo Martí was a Salvadoran revolutionary leader of the 1930s.

4. One night, during the time I spent with María in San José, she arranged a gathering for me to meet some of her close friends. She said she wanted me to talk to them about the book we were working on. It was at this gathering that I realized those present were also hearing the story of María's abduction and disappearance for the first time. They were shocked. Some were angry. I was stunned. María's inability to speak with co-workers of her experience had not been her only silence in this respect; she had also been unable to reveal it to close friends.

5. Shit. Whore. Damn it.

6. FIRE has also been broadcasting over the Internet since 1998 at www.fire.or.cr.

7. This comment was made by María in 1997.

SELECTED BIBLIOGRAPHY

Amnesty International. 1995. *It's about Time! Human Rights Are Women's Rights.* New York.

Askin, K. 1977. *War Crimes against Women: Prosecution in International War Crimes Tribunals.* New York: Kluwer Academic Publishers.

Bahar, S. 1996. "Human Rights Are Women's Right: Amnesty International and the Family." *Hypatia* 11, 1: 105–134.

Bennett, O., Jo Bexley, and Kitty Warnoc, eds. 1995. *Arms to Fight, Arms to Protect: Women Speak Out about Conflict.* London: Panos.

Bunch, Charlotte. 1990. "Women's Rights as Human Rights: Towards a Revision of Human Rights." *Human Rights Quarterly* 12: 486–498.

CODEHUCA (Commission for the Defense of Human Rights in Central America). 1992. *Centroamérica, escenario de "desaparición forzada": Cuadernos centroamericanos de derechos humanos.* San José, Costa Rica.

———. 1995. *La impunidad en Centroamérica: Causas y efectos.* San José, Costa Rica.

Cohen, G., and G. Thompson. 1995. "Unearthed: Fatal Secrets." *Baltimore Sun,* June 11–18.

Comisionado Nacional de Protección de los Derechos Humanos. 1994. *Los hechos hablan por sí mismos: Informe preliminar sobre los desaparecidos en Honduras, 1980–1993.* Tegucigalpa, Honduras.

Dorfman, A. 1998. *Heading South, Looking North: A Bilingual Journey.* New York: Farrar, Straus and Giroux.

Feitlowitz, M. 1998. *A Lexicon of Terror: Argentina and the Legacies of Torture.* New York: Oxford University Press.

Fisher, J. 1989. *Mothers of the Disappeared.* Boston: South End Press.

Fraser, A. 1999. "Becoming Human: The Origins and Development of Women's Human Rights." *Human Rights Quarterly* 21: 853–906.

Herman, J. L., M.D. 1992. *Trauma and Recovery: The Aftermath of Violence—From Domestic Abuse to Political Terror.* New York: Harper Collins.

Hollander, N. 1997. *Love in a Time of Hate: Liberation Psychology in Latin America.* New Brunswick, N.J.: Rutgers University Press.

James, S. 1994. "Challenging Patriarchal Privilege through the Development of International Human Rights." *Women's Studies International Forum* 17: 563–578.

Jelin, E., ed. 1990. *Women and Social Change in Latin America.* London: Zed Books.

Mellibovsky, M. 1997. *Circle of Love over Death: Testimonies of the Mothers of the Plaza de Mayo.* Willimantic, Conn.: Curbstone Press.

Soler, D. M. 1996. *El impacto psicológico de la repression política en los hijos de los desaparecidos y asesinados en Honduras.* Tegucigalpa, Honduras: Comité de Familiares de Detenidos-Desaparecidos en Honduras.

Thomas, Dorothy Q., and Michele E. Beasley. 1993. "Domestic Violence as a Human Rights Issue." *Human Rights Quarterly* 15: 36.

Ulriksen de Viñar, M. ed. 2001. *Memoria social: Fragmentaciones y responsibilidades.* Montevideo, Uruguay: Ediciones Trilce.

ABOUT THE AUTHOR

Margaret Randall has been listening to Latin American women tell their stories and been presenting those stories in text and image for more than forty years. For close to a quarter century she lived and worked in Mexico, Cuba, and Nicaragua (1961–1984) and has written many books about the people and movements of these countries, including *Cuban Women Now, Sandino's Daughters, Sandino's Daughters Revisited, Christians in the Nicaraguan Revolution,* and *Gathering Rage: The Failure of Twentieth-Century Revolutions to Develop a Feminist Agenda.*

Randall returned to the United States in 1984 and was soon after ordered deported, under the McCarran-Walter Act, for opinions expressed in some of her books. She and many supporters fought a four-year court battle, which she won in 1989. From 1985 to 1994, she was a visiting professor at Trinity College in Hartford, the University of Delaware, Macalester College, and the University of New Mexico.

Among Randall's more recent titles are *The Price You Pay: The Hidden Cost of Women's Relationship to Money, Hunger's Table: Women, Food, and Politics, Coming Up for Air,* and *Where They Left You for Dead / Halfway Home.* She lives with her partner, Barbara Byers, in the hills outside Albuquerque, New Mexico, and travels frequently to read and lecture.